# *Stepping Out on Faith*

# STEPPING OUT ON FAITH

*The Story of Colombia Missionaries*
*George and Helen Constance*

BY

# Helen Constance

CHRISTIAN PUBLICATIONS
CAMP HILL, PENNSYLVANIA

Christian Publications
3825 Hartzdale Drive, Camp Hill, PA 17011


The mark of ✝ vibrant faith


ISBN: 0-87509-409-0
LOC Catalog Card Number: 88-70986
© 1988 by Christian Publications
All rights reserved
Printed in the United States of America

# CONTENTS

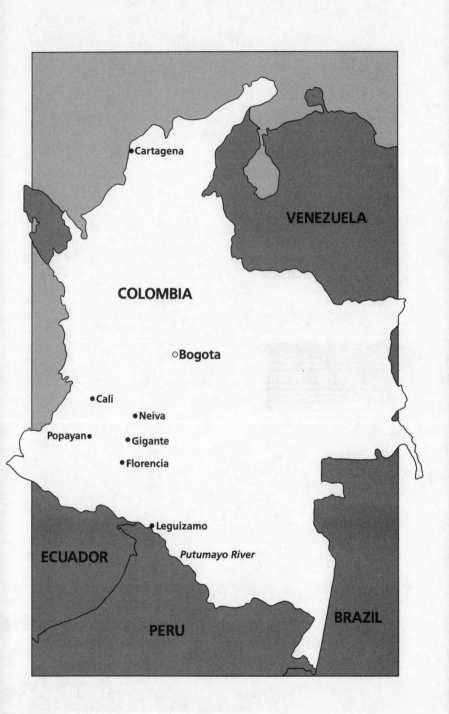

# FOREWORD

THE MANY, MANY PEOPLE who over the years have been captivated by Helen Constance's inspiring missionary addresses will not be disappointed by this gripping autobiography. It chronicles her pilgrimage—and that of her husband, George—from childhood and youth in rural Ohio through school, courtship and the sometimes horrendous difficulties as well as happy successes of pioneer missionary life in Colombia, South America.

Alexander Whyte once said of writing, "It is a true test of a work of genius that its touch fertilizes the mind of the reader." This book falls in that category. No matter how many other missionary autobiographies you may have read, this one is equal to the best. It is a life story told in an interest-riveting style. Along the way there are heart-tugging spiritual crises concerning the self-life as Helen faces stark loneliness, physical suffering and raw hardship amid primitive living conditions. She faithfully includes the shadows and poignant tensions alongside the joys of great victories.

And the reader, caught up in this unfolding story of Helen and her husband, who set themselves to live more truly the life that is hid with Christ in God, finds that their zest is infectious. The story inspires a new dimension of dedication.

I could wish every young person facing Christ's claims on his or her life would read this book. I wish every first-term missionary would read it. *Stepping Out on Faith* provides a much-needed perspective on life lived in obedience to Christ's call. Parents need to read it, too. It will "fertilize" their minds.

## 2 STEPPING OUT ON FAITH

Having known and appreciated George and Helen Constance over the years, I for one am most grateful that the story of their lives lived in the will of God is now available to a wide audience.

Louis L. King
Shell Point Village
Fort Myers, Florida
April 1988

# PREFACE

THROUGH THE YEARS I HAVE waited for a missionary of The Christian and Missionary Alliance to write a book about his or her experiences in Colombia. It has not happened.

Within my heart were many stories and spiritual experiences I longed to share. But I did not have the confidence that I could capture them in words. The insistent promptings of the Holy Spirit within my heart, however, demanded that I start clicking off typewritten pages, whether or not I had the ability to write.

Then, friends and relatives, getting along in years and cleaning out old memorabilia, began sending me letters they had kept — letters full of our experiences from long ago. God used those letters to jar me to my task.

Those letters, together with my own notes scribbled by flashlight in thatched huts after a day in the saddle or written as we traveled in a dugout canoe, merged with our vivid memories to tell the story of two people who answered the call of God to take the gospel, at any cost, to the "regions beyond."

My husband, George, has been my chief critic and my helper in this project. As he patiently "blue-penciled" my typed and retyped pages, sending me back to rewrite them once again, I appreciated the fact that we could be a team at the end of our lives as well as through all those years behind us. His suggestions and the double memory of our experiences made me glad that I could write this book while he is still alive.

It is to my beloved husband, George S. Constance, for whom I shall be eternally grateful, that I dedicate this story of our faith adventure together.

3

# CHAPTER

# 1

# *Letting Go*

T HE DILAPIDATED TRUCK, LOADED with our possessions, was at last ready for departure. Gingerly, I
mounted the front "seat"—a bench consisting of two
planks, one to sit on and one for a back rest. My
rangy husband, George, swung up beside me, and
with baby David soundly asleep in my arms, we were
on our way.

As we bumped along the potholed dirt road, the
fiendish planks were punishing, and conversation
was a shouting match above the noise of the ancient
motor. But with nine months of missionary experience in Colombia behind us, we were getting used to
such things. Besides, there was excitement in our
hearts as we thought of the challenge awaiting us in
Gigante (He GAHN tee).

Clouds of dust from the unpaved road whirled
around the open truck, tasting earthy on our tongues
and leaving grit in our teeth. We talked of the joy we
felt the week before during our first Colombian baptismal service. We laughed as we remembered the
curious crowd who had followed us through the tor-
rid streets of Neiva (NAY vah) to the nearby river.
Apparently they had never seen a folding baby

5

buggy — or a father pushing one. That was a woman's job!

We and the venerable visiting missionary, Homer Crisman, had not been the only objects of curiosity that day. The townspeople had been closely watching the lives of these believers. They were not about to miss this public baptism of the "evangelicals." We went single file down the narrow path to the water, singing all the way. The testimonies were thrilling! The new believers praised God that after years of spiritual darkness they had come to the light of the gospel.

"I was lost," one woman said, "but Jesus found me. I was full of sin, but He cleansed me with His blood. I was sick, but now I am healed. I was discouraged, but now I am happy in Jesus!"

Mr. Crisman and George had baptized 15 people. It was a first for George in Colombia, and he had savored every moment of the occasion. Had not Jesus promised, "Whoever believes and is baptised will be saved"? This was what foreign missions was all about!

Persuaded by the testimonies they heard at the baptismal service, a number of unbelievers had followed us to the service at the chapel that night. They would not enter, but they stood outside and listened to the unfamiliar but joyful singing. Though the believers were few, they gave forth a clear message as they sang, and Mr. Crisman's preaching was persuasive. In that pre-Vatican 2 era, they had been taught that it was a sin to possess a Bible and that only the Catholic clergy could interpret Scripture. (The Catholic attitude documented in this book changed significantly after Vatican 2 and the period of Colom-

bian history termed *La Violencia.*) Now we were saying that everyone should have a Bible.

As the truck climbed into the steep Eastern Cordillera, the road narrowed to a single lane. Occasionally we passed cave-like openings dug out of the
mountain, into which our driver sometimes eased
the truck to allow another vehicle to pass. But like
most rural Colombian truck drivers of 1936, ours
mainly relied on horn power to clear the road as he
whipped the vehicle around hairpin curves that
made us cringe in fear.

As we traveled toward our new home in Gigante
and a 200-mile district exclusively ours, we recalled
that day and praised God for the privilege of being
part of the "family" with those valiant believers, so
persecuted for their faith. Surely the service by the
river had given us new joy in the divine missionary
calling to which we both were committed.

It was 1928. The lanky young farmer gazed
proudly across the green fields of wheat and waving
corn that stretched beyond the hill. He was tired but
content as he caressed his new tractor with a rough
hand.

George Constance was a born farmer. For him no
other vocation compared with the thrill of working
the land. He knew the beauty of a summer dawn in
north central Ohio. He willingly rose in the dark of
winter to care for the livestock.

Everything was going well for George. He was ex-
panding and improving his livestock. He was acquir-
ing new equipment. It was only a matter of time
until the family farm, over which he was exercising
increasing responsibility, would be his.

As he headed toward the house in response to the supper call, his thick blond hair shown like a halo in the late afternoon sunlight. Six foot one and bronzed by the sun, he walked with the long, confident stride of a man who had found himself. The future was filled with dreams of the day when he would complete his agronomy degree at Ohio State.

There was but one cloud on George's horizon — something that had troubled him for years. He knew his parents were proud of his dedication to the farm, his obedience and his family concern. Yet he sensed their disappointment because of his indifference to religion. He knew their days began and ended with prayers for him, and he could not be completely comfortable in that knowledge.

George's parents had not always been devout, but when the change came, it was complete. The evenings of card playing and drinking were things of the past. Out had gone all the liquor, all the tobacco. Bible and church dominated their new lifestyle. Visiting pastors, missionaries and evangelists frequently were Sunday dinner guests. Often they stayed through the week.

One day while George was plowing, he stopped in the burning sun to drink from a jug of water. As he looked across the field, he saw walking toward him a man whom he recognized as a missionary guest in the home. Wary lest he be preached to, George dominated the conversation by talking enthusiastically about his future in farming.

Suddenly the missionary placed a strong hand on the younger man's arm. "George," he said, "some day you will be planting the gospel in a distant mission field. And the rewards of your labor will be far more satisfying than anything you have known here."

George laughed. He returned to his work thinking how mistaken the missionary had been. But nearly a year later, he still felt uneasy about that experience.

He was also ashamed about what had happened just that day. That afternoon, as he was plowing, he had struck a large stone, damaging the plow. In anger he let go a stream of curses. In the midst of his invectives, he heard a sound behind him and turned to see his mother, hurt written on her face. Never before had Jesse Constance heard him curse, and George knew it had cut like a knife across her sensitive soul. Silently she had met his eyes and held them for a long moment. Then she turned and walked away.

As he washed for supper that evening, he tried to avoid his mother. He knew he would face the usual question from his dad at the table: "Are you coming to prayer meeting with us, son?" All his weary body really wanted was food and rest, but he knew he would give the sought-after answer, "Sure, Dad." And to please his dad, he always went.

As the family bowed their heads for the blessing, George reflected on the tranquility of his home. Certainly he was privileged beyond measure to have parents like his, even if he did not agree with the religious fervor manifested in every phase of their lives. He had to admit that they lived the gospel they professed. They did not preach at him, but their lives were powerful sermons he did not especially want to hear. Though he obliged them by going to church, he sat in the back pew, anxious for things to end so he could return to his world of farming.

Sometimes from his back-pew vantage point, he would wonder how many of the congregation were praying for him. He had heard requests for "unsaved loved ones" too many times to doubt they included him. The fact made him uncomfortable. Deep in his heart he sensed an emptiness that even the farm could not fill.

Sunday evening, May 19, 1929, George sat in his usual place in the back of the church. The familiar hymns made no special impression on him, nor did the preacher's text and sermon. But as the invitation was extended, he felt a supernatural power pulling him toward the altar. He felt as if he was face to face with the claims of Christ. Perspiration poured down his face as he realized he was a sinner—a sinner being pressured by a holy God to decide what he would do about Jesus. His hands gripped the pew. His heart pounded. The congregation began to sing "Almost Persuaded."

Suddenly the young farmer rose and with long strides made his way to the front of the church. Throwing himself upon his knees, he wept uncontrollably as he prayed the sinner's prayer. When he got to his feet, he was at peace.

Much later that night, standing alone in the farmyard beneath a hemisphere of stars, George worshiped God. He rejoiced that his heart was cleansed, that he was God's child. Instinctively he knew that his life had changed irrevocably. His love for the farm must give way to the harvest fields Jesus spoke of when He said, "The laborers are few."

A new vitality surged through him as he walked around the homestead. He felt akin to Peter and John who in obedience to the Master's call left their nets and boats. He, too, was saying good-bye to his life's ambition so that he might answer God's higher call to missionary service.

Much later yet, as George was tip-toeing to his room, he met another family member too excited to sleep. Years of prayer and patient faith had at last borne fruit. There in the darkened hallway, father and son stood together, locked in a strong embrace.

Six years earlier, in Wadsworth, Ohio, 50 miles' distance from the Constance farm in Mansfield, my sister Gladys and I were dutifully absorbed in a gardening chore. Or, at least, 15-year-old Gladys was. We had been assigned by Dad to hand weed his long rows of corn. I, five years Gladys's junior, and possessed of a fertile imagination, was more interested in play. I would upend a handful of weeds and arrange them in a semicircle, roots in the air. These were my "school children."

"When children go to school, they must comb their hair," I softly chided my charges, carefully smoothing back the curly roots.

"Helen Powell!" Gladys's voice startled me, for I had not heard her approach. "I suppose those roots are the hair of your school children," Gladys continued indignantly.

Embarrassed, I returned to my weeding.

"Just remember, Helen Powell, when Dad comes home and your rows are not weeded, don't ask me for help!" Gladys strode back to her position far down the adjacent row.

Gladys—always so matter-of-fact, so industrious. And despite her ultimatum, I knew my later pleadings for undeserved assistance would not be denied.

That evening, Gladys pointedly said nothing to Dad about my unproductivity. But her motive was not totally pure. By threatening to break her silence, she had a ready whip, good indefinitely, to exact favors from me and to divest me of prized possessions.

Such expensive lessons notwithstanding, I could not suppress my powers of imagination. One of my duties was caring for the four Powell family members younger than I. I pretended they were students in my classroom. Many a conflict ensued because they rebelled against the teacher!

We had little time to play. But adjacent to our house was a field, and across the field was a large tree. Sometimes I retreated alone to that tree and, in its solitude, imagined myself a missionary in a far-away land.

### Changed Desire

Once I longed for beauty
    Of body and of face;
Now, I only want to know
    Christ's mercy and His grace.

Once I longed to be esteemed
    And have applause of men;
Now, I want above all things
    A heart that's free from sin.

Once I wished for talent rare
    To make Christ's message clear;
Now, I ask that needy souls
    Christ's voice, not mine, will hear.

Once I trusted in my friends,
    But this God taught me, too;

Only Christ and He alone
   Is constant, faithful, true.

Once I longed for power,
   Big things for Christ to do;
Now, I pray His Spirit will
   Fill me through and through.

Once I wanted to be loved,
   But now I clearly see;
I must give a dying world
   The love Christ gave to me.

Once I struggled hard to prove
   My battles I could win;
Now, my weary soul can rest
   On Christ who reigns within.

Once I thought I loved Him
   Until He let me see
My sinful heart — then broke it as
   I knelt at Calvary.

                    Helen Constance

CHAPTER
2

# Wadsworth — and Points East

THE BLEAK YEARS OF THE Great Depression were not favorable for starting new churches. Dad Powell had been soundly converted to Christ in the Bob Jones revivial of 1914. Ever since, his home had not been the same. Salvation had touched his wallet as well as his life. In addition to the tithe, he contributed regularly to missions and made other financial offerings to the church.

Family prayer at the end of the day was as inevitable as the setting sun. Each of us children was expected to pray as soon as he or she could talk.

The sight of Dad praying with tears running down his face made a deep impression on me. Dad often asked God to call at least one of his children to be a missionary. Watching him through our fingers, we older ones found it hard to understand why he should want us to leave beautiful America for a foreign land with its strange people and culture. But his prayer was to be doubly answered.

Dad was not only a spiritual leader in his own family. He was an excellent Bible teacher and lay preacher whom God used in area churches and open-air street meetings that were a part of religious life in those days.

In the small town of Wadsworth, there was an old abandoned building that set in a stand of chestnut trees. It was an uninsulated wooden structure with sawdust all over its dirt floor. Once it had been a meeting place of the Ku Klux Klan. Now a group of Christians began to meet there for worship, and Dad became the lay leader of that small band. He suggested that they become affiliated with The Christian and Missionary Alliance. He knew of a young man from Mansfield who was graduating from Nyack College. Perhaps the district superintendent could be approached about appointing him to be their pastor.

So it was that in early May 1932, George S. Constance came to Wadsworth to "look over the land." Had he been intent on material remuneration, he would not have unpacked his bags. The group could promise him no salary. They could not even rent an apartment for him. But fresh from his years of pastoral training at Nyack College, Pastor George decided to stay.

Dad was one of the few in the group who held a steady job through the Depression. His large home and garden were the only hope the church had for maintaining a pastor. Dad was anxious that this new group become a Christian and Missionary Alliance church. Although he already had many mouths to feed in his crowded home, he and Mother offered room and board to the new pastor.

Pastor George had a smile that warmed hearts and inspired confidence. He was witty, wholesome and without a lazy bone in his body. At once he set to work to get the rustic church building ready for the cold Ohio winter. Men without work volunteered their labor. Trees from the grove provided floor supports. They made a deal with a lumber company to pay $440 for matched pine flooring — payable at $10 a month. They piped in water for restrooms. They partitioned Sunday school classrooms at either end of the platform. Rebuilt furnaces provided heat. They installed new lighting, and George himself made benches for seating.

As the building took final shape, a pickup truck stopped near the front door. The driver was Pastor George's brother David, delivering a beautiful, hand-made pulpit — his gift to his brother's ministry.

After David had left, George encircled the lovely pulpit with his arms, put his head upon it and let the tears of gratitude and contrition flow. God had "lifted [him] out of the slimy pit, / out of the mud and mire; / he set [his] feet on a rock / and gave [him] a firm place to stand" (Psalm 40:2).

God had led him to his first church — meeting in a grove where a cult had once led people astray. He was there now to lead men and women to the Truth.

One of the challenges the new pastor at Wadsworth faced was the youth. His wit and fun-loving spirit endeared him to all of us. The times of happy fellowship as well as the regular Bible studies knit us together as a group.

Each week we went to a different home for evening prayer meetings. Since no cars were available, we walked — sometimes as much as five miles each way. In winter it meant snow-balling along the way.

In summer the walks were more leisurely, with pranks, singing and discussions enroute. Five of us Powell children were in the youth group, our ages 11 to 20. I was 20.

Our large kitchen became the youth hangout. Always hungry after meetings, we tried out our culinary skills. Pastor George's innovative cuisine and his ability to boss the cleanup so that Mother had no complaints kept him in the family's good graces.

Rapidly Pastor George was becoming an accepted member of our family. He was a merciless tease, but my younger brother Clyde, who was studying chemistry in school, reciprocated effectively with stink bombs that occasionally aroused the whole household. Each week Pastor George's brother David came for a visit—and to date me!

One evening Pastor George and I were discussing plans for a youth rally when he began speaking seriously about my going to college to prepare for missionary service. "Step out on faith!" he urged. I had never heard the phrase before. For the first time, I began to pray that God would provide a way.

When my letter of acceptance came from Nyack College, I felt a new kinship with Pastor George. I was filled with gratitude to God that He had sent just the right person into my life to encourage me in my walk with God.

The tall, stern dean of women scrutinized me, then consulted her chart. "You will be on the fifth floor," she announced. "It is a single room."

I could barely hide my disappointment. Nyack-on-Hudson, despite the area's incredible beauty, was a brand new world for a girl who had never ventured beyond the borders of Ohio. I had looked forward to having a roommate.

Simpson Hall (subsequently beautifully restored) had been built in 1897. The old stairs creaked as we carried suitcases up the five flights and set them in a tiny room with a supporting post right in its center. I looked at the splintery floor boards, the decrepit chair and desk, the small dresser. The curtainless window provided the only encouragement — a spectacular view of the Hudson River and Tarrytown, New York, on the opposite shore.

As I waved good-bye to my parents and pastor, I felt scared and incredibly alone.

The clanging of the breakfast bell the next morning urged me to join the excited cue of girls filling the stairways descending to the first-floor dining room. Upper-class girls embraced ecstatically while newcomers smiled timidly and hoped for new friendships.

At the table a tall girl from Toledo sat next to me and lamented that her baggage had been lost en route. She had only the clothes she was wearing. We laughed at the difference in our heights. Nothing I had would fit her.

That night the fifth-floor girls met for prayer. From then on, I was not lonely. As the weeks passed, a camaraderie developed that in some instances has lasted a lifetime. I was beginning to see that being alone enabled me to meet God in a way not possible if I had had a roommate. That tiny fifth-floor cubicle was becoming a special place of worship.

I had "stepped out on faith," as Pastor George said. Two part-time jobs were insufficient to meet my every material need. It was embarrassing to have to stuff cardboard into my shabby shoes—and uncomfortable when icy water seeped through. Clearly, it was time to trust God for a pair of shoes.

One day an announcement in the dining room informed us that shoes had been donated to the school. Anyone needing shoes should go to the designated room. Excited, I hurried to find the answer to my prayer. To my dismay, there was only one pair of size 5 shoes. They were orthopedic oxfords—old women's shoes! Reluctantly I slipped my feet into them. Alas! They fit.

Tucking the shoes under my arm, I mounted the stairs to my room.

"Lord," I prayed in tears, "You couldn't! You wouldn't!" But He had.

The next morning I wore them in a snowstorm and was glad at least for warm feet. I was ashamed of those shoes, but I thought it would be less embarrassing if I made fun of them. In class that day, I stuck out my feet and pointed to my shoes. The girls next to me began to laugh. Soon the whole row was snickering. Those ugly shoes brought me unexpected attention and lots of fun. I was impressed that God not only met my need but at the same time dealt with my pride.

The most exciting time of day at Nyack College was mail time. Girls working in the school post office lost no time in spreading word of the weekly "pastoral epistles" addressed to me. The letters from Pastor George kept me informed about the church, the family and what was happening in Wadsworth. He encouraged me to trust God for my needs and to seek God's best for my life.

The letters were casual and pastorly. Sometimes I wondered why my good-looking minister was so diligent in writing. It was embarrassing to be teased by the girls about those letters, especially since few of them received letters from their pastor. But his mature counsel was an encouragement to my faith.

When I returned for my second year at Nyack, I asked for my old room rather than a shared room on a lower floor. I had found my private times with God too precious to sacrifice to the benefit of human fellowship.

At the same time, as I looked forward to overseas missionary service, I was afraid to go alone. I knew the bravery of single missionary women, but my heart cry was that God would send me a husband to share my life.

I had to confess that I admired my handsome pastor. His personality charmed me, and I was impressed by his genuine dedication to the work of God. Certainly he was all a girl would want in a husband. Sometimes when the full moon made a golden path across the Hudson, I stood at my window thrilling at God's marvelous creation and remembering the walks with Pastor George and the Wadsworth young people as we went to our prayer meetings. Those times had provided much wholesome pleasure and rich fellowship. On occasion Pastor George had shown affection for me. But he had never broached marriage.

I knew Pastor George's three years of required North American work were coming to an end, after which he would qualify for an overseas appointment.

I had a warm feeling toward the man who had been used of God to help me "step out on faith." I knew that when the day came for him to leave, I would be very lonely.

One day a special delivery letter arrived for me. It was from Pastor George, and I hurried to my room to read it. If the missionary board was willing to waive my final year at college (at that time, the course was three years long), would I be willing to marry him and go overseas?

I knelt by my bed to weep in thankfulness and to pray for wisdom. My affections responded yes. But I felt so unprepared for the Lord's service. Friends had convinced me that I needed at least one year of nurse's training in order to be an effective missionary. I feared if I said yes I would not be the helpmate George needed.

I slept little that night. When the rising bell clanged the next morning, I awoke with a throbbing head. I knew I must answer George's letter. After several tries, I was satisfied. I assured him of my love and my pride in being asked to be his wife. I said I was certain the board would not accept me without the required studies and home service they deemed essential for missionary preparation.

George's reply informed me that he had already written the board requesting waivers. During the following month, the Dean of Women, college professors and officials from The Christian and Missionary Alliance headquarters interviewed me. They studied my records, reviewed my deportment and made their reports to the board. An official letter was my first inkling of the board's decision:

Dear Miss Powell:

You have been accepted as a missionary candidate of The Christian and Missionary Alliance. You will leave for Colombia, South America, in late 1935.

### A Missionary's Prayer

Shine on, my soul,
　　Let Christ shine forth so clear and strong
　　That in the darkness of earth's wrong
　　Transformed hearts break forth in song.
　　　　Shine on, my soul!

Shine on, my soul,
　　Remember that in sin's dark night
　　You felt the horror of death's deep blight,
　　Then someone led you to the light
　　　　That lit your path.

Shine on, my soul,
　　Shine in the city's noise and din
　　Where multitudes of hell-bound men
　　Rush on in hopelessness and sin
　　　　In Christless night.

Shine on, my soul,
　　Into that darkened grass-roofed hut,
　　And help that person from the rut
　　That superstition's fears have cut
　　　　Into his life.

Shine on, my soul,
　　Shine brightly on the jungle trail
　　Where Satan laughs at men's death-wail
　　And vows God's Truth will not prevail;
　　　　Shine in that night.

Shine on, my soul,
　　Let Christ in you a beacon be

That those around you clearly see
In Jesus all can be set free
    From Satan's grasp.

Shine on, my soul,
    Your light will never shine in vain
    As you press on in grief or pain
    Until the day when you shall reign
        Where Christ is light.

Helen Constance

(I wrote this poem as a missionary candidate looking at the stars from my fifth-floor window in Simpson Hall at Nyack College.)

CHAPTER

3

---

# New Horizons

HOW GLAD I WAS THAT I roomed alone when the letter arrived from Alliance headquarters! My emotions ran from hot to cold and back again. I was elated to think I would be the wife of my handsome, tall pastor. But as I thought of going out yet that year to missionary service in Colombia, fear overtook the joyful anticipation of marriage. My problem with an inferiority complex fell over me like a blanket. I struggled with fear and inadequacy.

When the girls met for prayer that night, I shared the contents of the board's letter with them. Their reactions were totally positive. They rejoiced that one of their classmates had been appointed to missionary service.

During the following days, as word spread of my missionary appointment, I was treated like a celebrity. It was impossible to study with thoughts of marriage and the gathering of a missionary outfit going through my mind. Some nights I could not sleep. I wondered if the board and the Lord could have made a mistake. Although untalented and inadequately prepared, I consoled myself in the knowledge that I would continue to learn to "step out on faith"—this time with my pastor!

One night God gave me a Scripture that was to be a lifelong challenge. It was from Isaiah 42:6–7:

> I, the Lord, have called you in righteousness;
>     I will take hold of your hand.
> I will keep you and will make you
>     to be a covenant for the people
>     and a light for the Gentiles,
> to open eyes that are blind,
>     to free captives from prison
>     and to release from the dungeon
>         those who sit in darkness.

I thought about my friends who would graduate the next year without me, and I envied them the year God asked me to forfeit for His sake. But the promise in Isaiah that I would be "a light for the Gentiles" could come true only as in obedience I let Christ shine within me.

Faithful parents, Sunday school teachers and pastors had let their light shine on my path. That light had brought me salvation and a changed life. Now, in turn, God was calling me to be a beacon shining in the dark places of Colombia. By His grace, I would be faithful.

The barn-like tabernacle in Wadsworth was not an elegant setting for a wedding. Hard times left us without money for flowers or other wedding accessories. So we planned a simple ceremony. A woman for whom I had done some work without pay kindly volunteered to take charge.

On the morning of the June 28 wedding, members of the congregation gathered armfuls of daisies from the fields. With them, they adorned the platform, the altar rail and the rough benches. We both borrowed our wedding attire—a gown for me and a suit for George. Somehow they seemed in keeping with our commitment to a life of sacrifice. George's recently rented apartment would be temporary home until our departure for Colombia.

The day was swelteringly hot, but that did not deter a capacity audience intent on witnessing the wedding of the tabernacle's young pastor. My bouquet shook and my heart pounded. When the officiating district superintendent paused for a breath, I answered "I do" ahead of time—a mistake my husband has never let me forget, claiming I could not wait to get him!

George's old car, piled high with camping gear, bore also some "Just Married" signs and a string of tin cans as we got away amid a shower of rice. The congregation, aware that we would be camping for our honeymoon at a nearby lake, thoughtfully gave us a food shower—all packed in the back seat of the car!

The tall preacher and his short wife were a study in opposites. Our dedication to Christ did not exempt us from a certain number of adjustments. A mirror, strangely enough, sparked the first argument of our marriage. On the second day of our honeymoon, I looked for the mirror and found it hung high on a tree, adjusted to suit a six-footer.

"Well, how in the world do you expect me to comb my hair with the mirror so high above my head?" I wanted to know.

"But what will I do if I put it on your level?" Suddenly we looked at the mirror and the tree and burst out laughing. It occurred to us at the same time that the solution was to have two nails—"his" and "hers."

Not all the problems would be resolved as easily, but we learned to respect each other's views.

With only five and a half months to raise our first year's support and travel expenses, we presented our needs in Christian and Missionary Alliance churches. As the money came in, we were impressed by the sacrifices of God's people. We prayed we would never disappoint them.

Because our commitment to missions had priority over our personal lives, we decided to delay any children for two years in order to give ourselves to language study and the adjustments to a new culture. But suddenly the smell of coffee or the sight of a fried egg sent me running to the bathroom. Prepared or not, I was going to be a mother!

The nausea that lasted all day weakened me, and Satan used it to instill fear. The prospect of taking a baby to unknown places where people had typhoid, yellow fever, malaria and parasites frightened me. I suggested to George it would be better to delay our departure until after the baby's birth. My husband's look of disappointment held a stronger message than did his reassuring words.

Two weeks before our sailing date, the pain in my back became so severe that I fainted several times. Consternation settled over our families. Although I was treated for a kidney infection, a week later I was so ill that George called headquarters for advice. They were sympathetic, but in effect they offered us the option of trusting God and going ahead with our plans or, lacking faith, waiting until we were cleared by our doctor. We had taken Christ as our Healer, and we decided to keep our sailing date. I was glad for the Rock-of-Gibraltar-kind of man I had married.

At our last meal with my family, everyone acted too cheerful. Beneath the fun there was the nagging feeling that we would never again be together in the same way. Dad, who had prayed for years that God would call at least one of his children to missionary service, never dreamed it would be the frailest of his seven. As he led in family prayer, he broke down. Sobbing aloud, he called on God to help him. Mother's tears also fell as in silence she watched us say good-bye to each brother and sister.

One of the joys of those days was our farewell from Nyack College. We could sense the students' enthusiasm for missions. The class in which I would have graduated seemed proud that one of their number was going forth. Their assurances of prayer support inspired our faith and courage. I climbed once more the squeaky steps to the fifth floor of Simpson Hall and stood in the little room where so many experiences with God had enhanced my life. I thanked God for Nyack College.

The day before we were to sail, I was examined by the headquarters doctor. Pain from the persistent kidney infection was still troubling me. The doctor immediately called the mission director and informed him that I was in no condition to travel. He advised that we cancel the trip until the infection cleared.

Our trunks were already on the dock. Our stateroom was reserved. The men at headquarters asked concerning our confidence in Jesus Christ, our Healer. They left the decision whether or not to proceed with us.

That God had directed our steps this far, we could not doubt. There was, for example, the "potato miracle" that provided the money for George's second year of college. He had tenderly cultivated his field of newly planted potatoes. And then July came with a burning heat that scorched the vines. The drought continued into August. Experienced farmers in the Mansfield area predicted a total loss. George returned to school convinced that only a miracle would resolve his financial problems.

And God answered prayer. It was not only a phenomenal pototo crop, but it was the *only* crop of potatoes that year in the whole county. Not only did it supply ample money for George's education, but it was a testimony that was not lost on the local farmers.

George and I reaffirmed our faith in God, committing ourselves and our baby to Him. We knelt as the officers of The Christian and Missionary Alliance laid hands on us and prayed. We had passed the point of no return. We were on our way.

Many of my classmates came to the dock to see us off. As we walked up the ship's gangplank, it was like cutting the umbilical cord to all that was familiar and dear. We stood at the railing as the vessel moved out of its slip. Far below us, relatives and friends were throwing kisses and tossing streamers. Already they seemed part of a different world.

We were still at the rail as the ship headed into the bay, past the majestic Statue of Liberty. George and I held hands and prayed, thankful that we had been commissioned to take Christ to those "living in darkness / and in the shadow of death."

# CHAPTER
# 4

# *Neiva, Our "Melting Pot"*

T HE ERA OF LANGUAGE SCHOOLS for Alliance missionaries had not yet come. In Colombia it was established that newly arrived missionaries go to Popayan to learn Spanish. Located in the Andes above the malaria line, Popayan's cool climate was conducive to study.

The missionary couple who preceded us had completed their year of language study by the time we arrived. We had been told the executive committee of our Colombia mission would assign them to another area for ministry, and we would move to Popayan to begin our year of study in that invigorating climate.

We were therefore unprepared to learn that the couple in Popayan had declined to move. They liked the city and had decided they wanted to stay right there. The mission had only one other house vacant at that time. It was in Neiva, a city much farther inland. Due to the intense heat, it would be far from ideal for language study. But George and I had sung

"I'll go where you want me to go, dear Lord." Like it or not, we accepted the assignment to Neiva.

The first leg of our trip would be by train. Nothing, absolutely nothing could have prepared us for the pushing and shoving as people struggled for a seat on the early morning train out of Buenaventura. Five people overflowed seats built for two. Others sat on the floor in the aisles. People balanced baskets on their shoulders. Babies cried. Frightened young children found themselves tossed about as the jerking train clanked and wheezed its way up the mountain. Through open windows, coal dust and cinders settled like a blanket over the passengers as the clattering locomotive strained to pull its cargo.

The hissing train stopped at every town. Vendors were on hand to push platters of hot chicken in the windows. Others offered fried plantain (cooking bananas) and native breads, their voices rising ever louder as they realized the foreigners did not understand the language.

Having been instructed not to buy street food, we were surprised when the missionary who accompanied us bought chicken legs covered with a yellow sauce, plantain and a beverage made undoubtedly from the unboiled water we had been advised not to drink. Heartened by the veteran's example, George pitched in and enjoyed every bite of the greasy meal, fanning away the insistent flies as he ate. I did not know it then, but I was to discover that my husband's stomach was made of cast iron. For the rest of his missionary life, he would hang out train and bus windows buying street food. Never did he have a gastronomical upset.

I, suffering already from morning sickness aggravated by the lurching of the train on the continuous curves, found it the part of wisdom to look the other way as the two men ate. It was not that I found Colombian food uninviting. I simply was not hungry.

Ruefully I regarded the white coat my mother had made for me as a farewell gift. It was gray with coal dust, streaked with black cinders and smeared by greasy little hands holding legs of chicken. *A white coat! How impractical,* I mused as I remembered with a lump in my throat the work my mother had put into her love gift.

Dear Mother. The Depression had driven her to develop skills unthinkable in former years. She made over cast-off clothing from relatives into charming dresses for the girls and serviceable pants and shirts for the boys. She supervised the canning that stretched our garden vegetables through the long winter months. She could half-sole a pair of shoes, mix cement or cut hair as efficiently as a professional—not to mention her ability as housekeeper and cook. How much I owed to my dear Mother!

It was dark when the train at last pulled into the city of Cali. Our field director, Homer Crisman, was there to meet us. The next morning, another train, with no better accommodations, took us to Armenia, where the Bible school was located. There we met several experienced missionaries. By contrast I seemed totally inadequate. I worried that I might never measure up to the task ahead.

"Lord," I prayed, "don't let them find out how weak, unprepared and scared I am." Long after George had fallen asleep, I lay awake praying for the little one within me, the strong man beside me and for the faltering, fearful person I was. There in the darkness, the words God gave to Joshua came to my mind: "Have I not commanded you? Be strong and courageous. Do not be terrified; do not be discouraged, for the Lord your God will be with you wherever you go" (Joshua 1:9). Renewed in spirit, I slept.

Travel by train had been a jolting introduction to Colombian culture. But at least it did not seem life-threatening. The same could not be said for our auto trip across the Andes. The driver with whom we contracted seemed determined to set a new speed record for the crossing or die in the attempt. The horseshoe curves whipped us so violently along the edge of precipices that all I could do was hang out the window in an agony of nausea.

There were certain places carved out of the mountain where the driver made brief comfort stops for passengers who had been pleading with him to "stop before I die." I hoped to *never* repeat the trip over the central Andes range again.

The next day, it was another train, and we fought our way through the crowd to get seats. Although the smoke and cinders again filled the passenger cars and soiled our clothes, this time the ride was smoother. Instead of mountainous curves, we looked out on a flat valley where naked children played near thatched-roof homes.

Homer Crisman had been a missionary for 40 years, and he would serve another 30 before retiring—a record for any Alliance missionary. He was the epitome of kindness and understanding, especially to me, the frail, frightened new arrival. He and his wife, Leticia, planned to remain with us in Neiva until we were adjusted and started in our language study.

Leticia served exotic dishes that she declared we would "love in no time." She instructed us how to treat a servant girl—social wisdom neither of us had had need for up to that point. To be served at the table? To have our laundry done for us—by hand on a cement slab? There were times in the years that followed when I was sure it would be easier to do those tasks myself than to work with someone whose culture was so different. But language study and the absence of labor-saving appliances made such household help a necessity.

For two action-oriented people like George and me, it was difficult to spend most of each day learning vocabulary words and studying a Spanish grammar. The pain in my kidney further dispelled any latent enthusiasm I might have mustered. I was a willing worker, but I lacked the strength to accompany George and Homer as the latter introduced my husband to the groups of believers in the district.

Our new home was comfortable. The bedroom had a large, barred window that opened onto the sidewalk. Grass grew in the middle of the unpaved street. Donkeys grazed in the patches of green. Often they would frighten us by braying before dawn beneath our window.

When the curtains were open in the daytime, faces peering in the window gave us the uneasy feeling of always being watched. In those days, foreigners were a curiosity in the interior of Colombia.

After a month, the Crismans left for other ministries, and we were alone. The heat was exhausting, and the sand flies caused red welts that itched unbearably. For some unknown reason, they did not bother George, but they were a trial to me. In desper-

ation I searched through our barrels for the cotton
stockings that some dear saints thought all missionaries wore. These I pulled over my arms and legs.
They discouraged the pesky insects, but I looked
ridiculous, and in the heat they added their own
dimension to my misery. Eventually, after months of
distress, I became somewhat acclimated to sand flies,
and they bothered me less.

Having our home to ourselves spurred me to the
challenge of cooking the Colombian way. Interesting
and sometimes strange concoctions resulted. I
thanked God for a husband who could eat anything
and enjoy it. Often I did not!

The outside shower provided little relief from the
heat since the pipes were above ground and became
sizzling hot in the sun. The privy attracted cockroaches, snakes, scorpions and millions of mosquitos.
We never went there at night without a flashlight.

The Neiva believers were a great encouragement.
Faithfully they turned out to listen to a preacher
they could not understand. They would smile ap-
provingly while their *gringo* pastor butchered their
beautiful language, afterward remarking how well he
spoke.

One of my most trying experiences as a new missionary came when I tried to fill the gap left by a
musical predecessor who could make the little folding organ at the church sound like a mighty Wurlit-
zer. Since we knew that singing would always be a
large part of our ministry, Geroge insisted that I take
time each day to learn to play the organ. Day after
day I worried my way through the simplest hymns.
George accommodatingly chose only hymns I knew.
Even then I could not keep up with the congrega-

tion. Many times they finished the song while I was still hunting the notes. I wanted to die! But the loving believers loved us in spite of our blunders, expressing their affection in many ways.

Eventually competence at the organ finally came, and I thanked God for a husband who pushed me to develop the requisites for an effective ministry.

As the baby within me developed, the pain in my side became constant. Our plan was to return to an American clinic on the other side of the mountains for the delivery. Because the crossing was so difficult, we agreed to travel at least a month before the baby was due. I was counting the days. Meanwhile, our confidence in the Great Physician held us steady. We had the supreme comfort of Paul's inspired words in Colossians 1:27: "Christ in you, the hope of glory." The security of our commitment to Him brought peace as we prepared for lifelong missionary ministry. The faithful believers in Neiva, who endured persecution and ridicule for Christ's sake, inspired us to see that beyond the language barrier there were multitudes who needed to know Jesus, whose indwelling presence was their one "hope of glory."

## Christ in Me

"Christ in you, the hope of glory"—
  What a blessed truth for me!
In my heart He deigns to govern
  And like Him some day I'll be.

He lives within to give me wisdom,
  Helping me choose right from wrong;
He controls my thoughts and actions,
  Puts within my heart a song.

Christ within—when pain and sorrow
   Pierce my soul and tear my heart;
In my own Gethsemane
   He is there—our place apart.

"Christ in me"—when darts from Satan
   Hurt my body, try my soul,
His truth the shield, protecting, keeping,
   Making broken body whole.

"Christ in me"—when I am weary
   As I walk my rugged way,
Jesus takes His place beside me,
   Giving grace for each new day.

"Christ in me"—oh, help me live it
   With a glad vitality!
That the world may see the beauty
   Of the living Christ in me.

Helen Constance

# Surprise!

I︎T WAS ONE O'CLOCK IN THE MORNING. The date was
March 31, 1935. In our Neiva bedroom the heat
was stifling. I found sleep impossible under the re-
strictive canopy of mosquito netting.

The snores emanating from the other side of the
bed united with the heat to evict me into the suffo-
cating living room. There was not the slightest
breeze from the window. As I paced the floor, insects
hummed and an occasional birdcall broke the silence
of the night.

This pain was different.

By now I had learned not to bother my husband
because of pain. So I walked and prayed—and wondered. Finally, at two o'clock, desperate and afraid, I
awoke George. He dutifully got up, gave me aspirin,
sleepily mumbled words of comfort and stumbled
back to bed, soon snoring comfortably, totally unaf-
fected by the heat.

At three, I awoke him again. More aspirin. Back to
bed for George.

By four, I was certain the baby had no intentions
of waiting for us to cross the Andes. Desperately my
husband pulled on his clothes and went into the
darkness in search of a doctor. There was no tele-

phone. Since no one was in the streets at that hour, he could not ask directions to the only address he had.

At last George discovered the residence of a doctor. The man put his head out the window, listened to the broken Spanish of the *gringo* and slammed the shutter.

As the faint rays of a new day brought people into the streets, George sought their help. Suspicious of this *Protestante* whom they conjectured might be a Communist as well, they angrily turned away.

At last, shortly before six in the morning, a doctor listened, dressed and accompanied George to the home where a desperate mother-to-be, writhing in pain, waited. The doctor gave me a quick examination and turned to leave, predicting it would be hours before the baby arrived. But when he bent over me to console me, I grabbed his necktie and gasped that the baby was coming *now*. Hurriedly he delivered a three-pound baby boy who was blue and weak but screaming.

What a scramble! We had packed a suitcase of baby things in anticipation of our trip over the mountains to the clinic. But some needed things were still in our steel barrels. As the doctor barked orders, the servant girl ran from kitchen to bedroom fulfilling his demands. George busied himself getting the folding baby carriage from its crate and with trembling hands managed to get it set up. Meanwhile, the doctor wrapped David Charles Constance in a blanket and laid him on the table, neglecting him entirely as he cared for me. Later, he admitted that he did not expect the baby to live.

When the moment at last came for tiny David to

be placed in my arms, my joy was beyond expression. What a marvel it was to be a mother! George was exuberant. He held that tiny son of his — not much longer than his hand — with wonder and pride. Our elation, however, was tempered by the knowledge that only a divine miracle would let that three pound bit of humanity survive without incubator and special help.

The doctor promised to send a nurse. She arrived an hour later. The image in our minds was far different from the person who came. She was a typical Indian, dressed in the garb of the poor. She had been trained by the doctor to help in such cases, but her demeanor inspired no confidence in us.

The nurse understood no English, and we understood little Spanish, so we let her proceed as she wished. I was too ill to be of much help anyhow. She wrapped David in cotton wool from head to toe, then in blankets. Then she placed him in the baby carriage. In that heat we wondered if he could possibly survive.

David was too weak to nurse and had to be fed by hand. The process of taking the milk, then warming it was unique. The nurse soaked cotton in alcohol, placed it on the brick floor, lit it and held the pan of milk over the blue flame. She then fed the warm milk to our baby with a spoon. Every two hours, night and day, this ritual was repeated, exhausting all of us — especially me. The nurse seemed atypically concerned about germs. On everything — wash basin, bedpan and even soap dish — she poured alcohol and put a match to it. We feared the room would go up in flames with the germs!

In desperation, George wrote to another mission

to see if we might get the help of a trained nurse. We were heartened when a British nurse arrived at the end of the week.

In the meantime, the little Indian woman with her primitive ways cared for me and the baby. The doctor, who stopped by to note progress, agreed with his nurse's methods. In spite of the differences in language and culture, the Colombian nurse gained our love. After the English nurse came, our Indian friend returned often to visit. Such a tiny baby as David should not have been moved. But the Indian carried him around, showing him off to everyone, proudly displaying her affection for the little *gringo*.

Our nurse from England stayed for a month. Then we were alone again in one of the most trying times of our lives. The oppressive heat, our frail little baby and a sick wife were not what George had expected when he answered God's call to missionary service. All those plans of active missionary work with half days for language study had to be set aside in the sheer struggle to survive.

As for me, the demands were overwhelming. I was feeding the baby every two hours, trying to run the home with the help of a girl we could not understand and giving attention to nationals who came by needing help. And always there nagged at me the comparison of my feeble efforts with those of the experienced missionaries who preceded us.

We had been somewhat prepared for opposition to the gospel, but we were unprepared to be actually hated. It was totally contrary to anything in our past experience. If we were out walking, it was not uncommon for teenagers to come up behind us, shouting, "*Abajo con los Protestantes!* (Down with the Protestants!)" In the market people stared at us coldly. Some vendors refused to sell to us. Our church services were regularly interrupted by a rain of stones thrown on the chapel roof. We had to do some heart searching about the depth of our commitment to missionary work.

David's demands on me left little time for the language study I so desperately needed. The devil reminded me that I would have done better to stay in the United States if all I could do was be a wife and mother. I was not gaining strength, and the condition that brought on the baby's premature birth was still with me.

I thought back to the many missionary women I had heard speak. I could not recall even one telling of discouragement like mine. All of them seemed to exude victory. I had the impression that just being a missionary was sufficient to make Satan back away.

I wept because I could not measure up to the ideal I had set for myself. I loved the Colombians, and with my limited vocabulary, I expressed myself as best I could, supplementing what I said by a smile and the customary *abrazos*—hugs. But I longed to have greater fellowship with the believers and to truly minister to those who did not know my Savior. Yet I felt so foreign—so unable to express what was in my heart and mind. Sleepless nights, the heat, the mosquitoes, the concern for David enveloped me in clouds of depression. I wondered if anyone back home was praying for us.

After some months, we were visited by a missionary who insisted on taking me to a doctor. The doctor examined me thoroughly, then talked frankly with George and me. He told us I was too weak to endure the heat of Neiva. He doubted that I would ever be able to live in the tropics. He concluded it would be best for us to return to the United States.

That evening the missionary who had insisted on my seeing the doctor, talked with me. "I can't understand why the board ever sent you," she said.

I was devastated! I had received a verdict about myself from a veteran worker who probably was right. I thought about my strong husband whose Spanish was improving daily. I thought of the great ministry he could have in the years ahead, and I dared not think of his giving that up because of me. Right there I determined never to concede, doctor or no doctor. My call was definite, and God's promises were worthy of trust. I would go forward. I would be my best for Him.

Fortified by that resolve, I ventured forth alone one day to make a purchase. At the store the clerk not only returned my smile but she understood what I said in Spanish. I felt triumphant! But on the way home, a group of boys came up behind me shouting the hated phrase "Down with the Protestants!" They began to throw pebbles, which stung my legs as I quickened my pace toward home.

Once inside the house, I flung myself into a chair and sobbed uncontrollably. It was not that my legs hurt, but my pride was crushed. I remembered the satisfied smirk on the faces of the two upper-class women as I experienced that degrading trial on the street. Anger filled me. With clenched fists, I beat the arms of the chair. "I don't have to take it! I don't have to take it!"

Immediately, an inner voice seemed to say to me, "I took it for you." Slowly, the anger abated and I felt ashamed. I saw in my mind my Lord being beaten and crucified for a lost world. Yet in all His suffering, He "did not open his mouth." The mental vision brought such a rebuke that I tearfully yielded myself once again for whatever God had for me. With renewed commitment, I placed my life in God's care and prayed for healing and the ability to suffer for Christ's sake.

# *Alone*

ONE DAY GEORGE SAID HE FELT led to make a trip south to the small town of Gigante, about 40 miles from Neiva. The climate in Gigante was cooler, and he believed God wanted him to find a healthier location for his family.

We loved the Christians in Neiva. We would ever be grateful for their tolerance and loving acceptance of us. It would be hard to leave them. But God had given us a new responsibility, too—a son to raise for His glory. We had dedicated David to God, and Paul's words in Second Timothy 1:12 became our confidence: "I know whom I have believed, and am convinced that he is able to guard what I have entrusted to him for that day." Watching David with his big brown eyes and captivating smile, we praised God for the joy our son brought to us in the midst of the hard adjustments to missionary life.

George's main problem in Gigante was finding someone who would rent to Protestants. We were considered heretics and, as such, a curse to the community. But George finally managed to locate a house to rent. And so it was that we found ourselves in the ancient truck on our way from Neiva to Gigante, the memory of newly baptized believers in Neiva a benediction upon our nine months of ministry in that small city.

The house where we would live for the next five years was typical of the area. It was of adobe construction with two-foot-thick walls and brick floors. The bricks were not cemented in but simply laid over the ground. No matter how often I swept, the dirt from between those bricks filled the dustpan.

An old sofa had been left in the living room, and we added two locally made cowhide chairs and a small table. The large bedroom, when furnished, contained the frame George had made to hold our mattress, a few boards nailed together for a closet for our clothes (with a colorful curtain to hide them), a rocking chair and a homemade dressing table. We ate our meals in the outside corridor that also served for our church services.

The kitchen was a disaster! A huge baked-mud oven dominated the room, but we used our kerosene stove and small oven instead. A counter made of bricks served as working space. The rafters as well as the walls were black from the smoke of open fires. The kitchen was the most primitive part of the house — something true of all Colombian small-town homes at that time.

Bamboo canals brought water from a nearby stream to our back yard, where it emptied into a cement tank. Boards around this tank afforded some privacy to bathe, though I worried about the spaces between the sun-shrunken boards. And we soon discovered that water snakes occasionally made their way down the canal into the tank.

From the bamboo canal, we hand carried water to

the kitchen. The canal's overflow ran under our out-door privy.

If the home was not modern, its setting was beautiful. Located on a cliff above a small river that wound its way along our property and under a bridge, it provided a view of the only road into town. Women washed clothes in the river, pounding them against the rocks, then spread them on the grassy banks to bleach. Near the cliff two beautiful trees standing close together overlooked the river. Scores of orchids clung to the branches of the trees, their year-round blooms providing a luxury we never would have know in the States. Across a narrow valley, a great mountain formed a delightful back-drop.

It was a relief to be in the cooler climate. All of us slept better, and language study was easier. Believers came in from the country each Sunday to meet in our open-air corridor. With no missionaries or national workers to help us, our limited Spanish was pressed to capacity. George labored over his sermons and I, my Sunday school lessons. The people encouraged us by saying we spoke better Spanish than they did. Knowing differently, we accepted the compliments but determined that each day would bring us closer to fluency.

The town priest condemned the man who had rented to us and warned the faithful not to have anything to do with the Protestant missionaries. Some market vendors, in compliance, would not sell to us. We were watched suspiciously whenever we walked the streets. As in Neiva, stones would rain on the roof during our services, drowning out the preacher's voice. At such times I played the little organ, and we sang until the disturbance ceased.

Little by little, however, as we visited the sick, sent gifts after funerals and shared the people's problems, we were able to establish friendships. Upper-class townspeople could not understand why we were not ashamed to be seen with the poor and despised evangelicals. In their eyes, the evangelicals were socially ostracized. People frequently commented to us that a priest had never visited them or their family.

At Christmas, we delighted in cards and letters from home. A 20″ artificial Christmas tree and a few gifts arrived from the States. I eyed the monstrous mud oven in our kitchen and considered the possibility of using it to cook our Christmas dinner. My pre-Christmas trial run was a failure. So we asked a Colombian expert to show us how to fire it properly. He filled the oven with wood, burned the wood to ashes, then swept everything clean. That done, he put my casserole and homemade bread into the still-hot cavern, and both turned out fine.

On Christmas day, the oven was fired by a novice—George. But he must have done it right. The turkey, vegetables, rolls and pies were deliciously baked. Fellow missionaries spent the day with us, and David was thrilled with the tree and gifts. For all the rest of our years in Colombia, Christmases were given over to several days of special meetings for the Christians. But this first Christmas in Gigante, except for a Christmas Eve service, was a family occasion. We savored it then, and we have recalled it fondly ever since. Despite our happiness, however, we could not help but think of our families in the States and of happy Christmases in years gone by.

Christmas in Colombia, unlike at home, received

scant notice from the general populace. Easter was—
and is—the big holiday in Colombia. Easter brought
to us a new insight into the spiritual darkness that
surrounded us. Priests led long processions of people
carrying statues of the saints followed by others with
lighted candles. There was the pageantry of Christ's
crucifixion, recreated with every gruesome detail.

After the self-denial of Lent, the people gave full
vent to their vices. The revelry, drunkenness and debauchery revealed both the darkness of their hearts
and the superficiality of their religious beliefs. Men
on horseback reeled drunkenly down the streets,
scattering frightened people before them. Mountain
folk filled the plaza and the streets, spending their
last *centavos* on liquor in hopes of forgetting the
wretched poverty of their lives.

But for the few believers who walked the trails for
hours to celebrate Easter with other like-minded
Christians, it was a time of rejoicing. George kept his
sermons short, giving most of the time to singing and
testimonies. He encouraged the people to learn what
God was doing in others' lives. And the several unbelievers who reluctantly accompanied their friends or
relatives to the services returned home with portions
of the Scriptures and a desire to know more about
the evangelical way.

The Easter services brought a sense of triumph.
Neither George nor I was fluent in Spanish, but we
were making progress. Our living situation was an
improvement over hot Neiva. David was progressing
normally. I dared to feel encouraged.

And that was when George announced he was
going to make a three-week trip to a mountain town
called San Vicente. At that time there were no roads

to San Vicente, so he would travel on horseback, visiting en route other villages nestled in the Andes. George took it for granted that being away for three weeks would be readily accepted by his wife. But George's wife panicked!

"You mean you are going to leave me alone with only a native girl as helper for three whole weeks?" I protested. "Who is going to teach the adult Sunday school class? Who will preach the Sunday sermons?"

"You will have to do those things," George replied. "You know that no national workers are available at this time. You are able to do it." George tried to pump some confidence into me.

"It is imperative that I go," my husband continued. "Remember, the Lord's work is first, even though I hate to leave you."

I reflected on my interview with the board at Nyack and a question that had been put to me. "Miss Powell," one of the members had asked, "will you be willing to let your husband go on trips of one or two months, leaving you alone?" Ruefully, I thought how easy it had been to answer affirmatively then; how hard it was when the test actually came. I was positive that I was not ready to be thrust into the role of teacher and preacher even for three weeks. The hostility of the townspeople was tolerable as long as George was present, but being alone when rocks rained on the roof presented an entirely different situation. I shared George's burden for the many communities without the gospel, but I tried to convince him that the time was not yet ripe for such a trip.

When my pleadings were to no avail, I became angry. That anger stayed with me to the last minute.

I felt I was being abandoned by my husband. But as I kissed George good-bye, I realized my fear was greater than my anger.

I watched George ride away, sitting tall and handsome on his horse, with only a blanket, a change of clothes and a few other necessities tucked into the saddlebags. Behind him he led a mule ladened with Bibles and gospel literature. Suddenly my heart melted and tears flowed—as they were to do many times in the days just ahead. Earnestly I sought forgiveness for my bad attitude as I prayed for my husband's safety. With renewed dedication, I surrendered to God my unwillingness to let my husband go.

Lonely nights provided time to prepare for the tasks ahead. I gave every available minute to the preparation of Sunday school lessons and messages. Sunday came, and with fear I faced the people. But as I began to speak, I lost myself in the divine truths of God's Word. I was aware of my inadequacy in the language, to be sure. But the positive response of the people and the satisfaction within my own heart buoyed my spirits.

The lessons I learned during those three weeks of separation would benefit me the rest of my missionary life. It was never easy to have George leave. Many times there was a battle within my heart. Had my husband pampered me, I probably never would have developed the ability to speak in public. Time and again when I felt the task before me was overwhelming, George's insistence that I could do it built my confidence in a God whose declared policy is to choose "the weak things of the world to shame the strong."

Meanwhile, George was learning some lessons, too — lessons much harder than mine. He traveled nine hours a day, eating food prepared under primitive conditions. He slept on dirt floors, in hammocks, on planks, on outdoor trays made for drying coffee beans. He endured the heat of the day and the cold of night. Often he had no place to bathe. Mosquitos and ticks made him miserable. And he missed his family.

At night, although dead tired, he led meetings by candlelight or lantern in thatched homes filled wall to wall with people anxious to hear what the missionary had to say. The joy of giving them the Word of God and finding a response in many of their hearts was worth the misery and hardship. All along the trails he witnessed in homes and towns tucked into mountain recesses. That trip and the many others that followed would bring forth much fruit in later years. Groups of believers that began meeting in homes were subsequently able to build churches. From those churches young people came to the Bible school to prepare for Christian ministry.

It was a glad day when the clop-clop of a horse's hoofs sounded on the cobblestone entrance to our home in Gigante. What happy embraces! What joyful rehearsals of all that God had done for both of us! Each of us was filled with new enthusiasm for our missionary work. God had proved to us that He was bigger than any trial that would touch our lives.

That evening a happy little boy fell asleep in his daddy's arms, and the sweet presence of God permeated our home. With David tucked into bed, George and I, arm in arm, stepped out into the moonlight that bathed house and yard in its peaceful glow. The towering mountain silhouetted against the vast sky spoke to us of the unchanging omnipotence of our God. Innumerable times those Andean peaks to which we lifted our eyes would remind us that our help came "from the Lord, / the Maker of heaven and earth."

## Looking Up

O God, I stand in awesome contemplation
    Before the Andes towering high above;
The eternal snowcaps gleaming far beyond me
    Speak forcefully of Your creative love.

Those ragged peaks that reach out to the heavens
    Immutable have stood through ages past;
So You, O God, unchanging in Your promise,
    Will one day welcome me in Heaven at last.

The scrambling trails that press forever upward
    Along the cliffs to dizzy, breathless height,
Remind me that as life's steep trail I follow
    You alone can guide my steps aright.

King of the Andes, the great majestic condor,
    Leaves rocky cliffs the valleys to explore;
But nature calls him back to soar the heavens —
    His habitat the heights forever more.

So, while my soul must live within the valley,
    Insistent is the call to peaks above,
To soaring heights beyond the world's false glitter
    Where I can rest in Christ's unchanging love.

The blue sky as it contrasts with the mountain
    Covered with the green of forest trees
Causes me to worship You in wonder
    And send this prayer upon the evening breeze:

"My God, the great omnipotent Creator,
   The beauty of Your handiwork I see;
My soul, inspired and contrite, weeps in worship.
   Oh, wonder of it all! 'Twas made for me!"

But greater than the splendor of creation
   Of sun and moon and stars—or rolling sea—
Is Calvary, where God's own Son was offered
   To shed His blood and set my poor soul free.

Helen Constance

The ancient truck, loaded with our household effects, is about to start off from Neiva for Gigante. I'm standing with David in my arms not far from the driver.

"Don Jorge," pack mule loaded, is ready to mount his white charger and set out on one of his many missions into the mountains.

This was our house on the cliff in Gigante. We held church on an L-shaped veranda on the other side of the building.

These workers are ready to give our bamboo-framed school room at Gigante its first coat of mud-and-manure plaster.

David is on my lap in this picture of our school students at Gigante. The teacher is the man with jacket and dark tie.

Two of our Gigante students who went on to positions of church leadership were Jael (left, pictured with her husband), who became the first national WMPF president, and Solomon (right, with family), who was named president of the Colombian C&MA.

I'm third from left in this pose with our older school girls in Leguizamo. As you can see, some were taller than I!

This was our Colombia missionary field staff in 1953. The picture was taken at the time of our annual conference. George is seated third from left, and I am next to him in the polka dot dress.

# "Let the Children Come"

ONE MORNING MY HUSBAND ANNOUNCED at breakfast that it was time I learned to ride a horse. Most of the rural Colombians lived on small farms scattered throughout the mountains or in villages accessible only by trail. Having been raised on a farm, George found horseback riding second nature. I had never ridden, but I was eager to learn.

As I stood beside it, the steed George had selected for my initiation looked 10 feet tall. I quickly discovered that the stirrups, adjusted for my short legs, were too high from the ground for me to mount the animal. Our Colombian helper hurriedly put a chair beside the horse, and I stepped first onto the chair, then into a stirrup, and then I swung my other leg over the long-suffering beast.

George gave me the reins, and my horse followed his from our yard to the unpaved street. Not until we started down the road did I realize what a contrast we were. George was a knight in shining armor sitting on a white, young prancer. I came behind on an old nag whose head hung low as he lumbered along

57

like a pack animal. The scene was so unusual that citizens came to their doors to watch us pass. I was especially conscious of their stares and not a little embarrassed. I felt like a peasant wife.

"Why am I riding on this old nag while you sit like a king on a white charger?" I demanded.

George was conciliatory. "Honey," he answered, "I would not dare put you on a spirited horse until you learn to ride." I soon began to feel the impact of what he meant. As George's horse picked up a faster pace, mine loped along, causing me to hit the saddle with rhythmic jolts. It was misery.

When we reached open road outside the town, it was difficult for George to rein his horse to a walk. Though only trotting, my horse's every step brought me excruciating pain, as though my innards were all being thrust into my rib cage. My awkwardness as a novice made me determine I would learn to ride well whatever the cost. But the next morning, when just getting out of bed required divine help, I had second thoughts.

The neglected mountain people were amazed that a Protestant minister would visit them. Their contact with the Catholic church was limited to their trips into town. No priest ever came to them. They carried their dead in crude coffins over the rough trails to the in-town church, where they paid with produce or other possessions for the priest's blessing. They were pressured to give for endless masses in the dim hope of getting the deceased out of purgatory. And as a result, they were always in debt to the church. When they asked George to bring his wife to visit them, I determined that regardless of aching body I would ride that trail.

Later, my apprenticeship behind me, I remember early morning rides across the wide, golden valley from town to foothills. Sometimes we would give our horses full reign over that long stretch before the slow, steady climb began. Often we held hands as we rode side by side. The rhythm of the horses and the exultation in our hearts provided vigor and excitement that no worldly pleasure could possibly have offered.

As David grew, he often shared one of the saddles with us. He loved to pass out gospel tracts, and even the most fanatical people could not resist his smile and his literature.

Increasingly, people began to confide in us. Our large L-shaped porch was not only the place of worship, but a place where the townspeople came to share the sadness of their lives and to seek spiritual guidance. We were shocked to discover how many couples were not married, though they parented new babies year after year. Frequently these common law husbands would totally abandon their partners and children, going elsewhere in search of employment, leaving the women to raise the children alone.

Even the men who remained with their families considered it *macho* to spend their evenings at the town bar. Women told me of the beatings and abuse they suffered as a result of the nightly drinking. These women could not help but note our happiness, and they marveled that George enjoyed being with his family. Tears flowed as I pointed them to Christ and urged them to read the Gospels. George talked with the men about their responsibilities to their families and about the deliverance from sin that only Christ can give.

Little by little, our congregation grew. Men who for years had been slaves to alcohol were converted and brought their families to church. These families reached out to relatives and friends living in the mountain villages. House churches resulted as the many small groups began calling themselves evangelicals. We were grateful for the help of colporteurs and visiting Colombian evangelists who could assist in the work.

The mountain believers suffered some of the same harrassment we had experienced. They were ostracized in their communities. Some were dismissed from their jobs. People refused to buy their coffee beans, cakes of rock-hard brown sugar, firewood or whatever else they had to sell at market. They were excommunicated from the Catholic church. Yet amid poverty and discrimination, they testified to an inner peace that made it all worthwhile.

The children were mainly my responsibility. Sunday school gave me the joy of teaching them gospel songs and verses of Scripture. Flannelgraph was new and fascinating to them, and they were never restless during the Bible story. Discipline was never a problem. In the local culture even the most underprivileged child had been taught to respect adults.

Our greatest heartache was for the children. One morning I awoke to a baby's cry outside our door. There I found a six-year-old child holding her infant sister, four months old, trying to stuff a strong citrus fruit into her mouth. The girl said her mother took the three other children with her to the river, where she washed clothes for a living. But as the eldest, she had the job of finding food for herself and the baby. My mother heart was filled with compassion. These were responsibilities far too great for a thin, neglected child of six. I bathed and fed them, but I grieved at the end of the day when I had to send them back to what was called home.

That scene was repeated many times in different ways. I longed to start an orphanage and take them all in. How many missionaries, I reflected, must have struggled with this tremendous problem. For a time I fought bitterness because our mission refused to become directly involved in the social betterment of people. Yet, realistically, I had to face the fact that we were not equipped to feed the world. Our purpose was to evangelize the world, not to sustain it physically.

At least, that was the rationale. Abiding by it was not so easy. Especially when two little girls, three and five years old, were found alone in an abandoned house. Their mother had died, and their father had taken off with another woman, leaving the girls to fend for themselves. A believer brought the two to me.

The children were in pitiable condition. I bathed them, fed them, treated their skin rashes and head lice and made dresses for them. What a delight it was to see them in Sunday school, so pretty in their new clothes! But our meager living allowance barely covered our own necessities, so we persuaded a relative to take them. It was an extremely poor home, and I never heard of them after the family moved away.

It hurts to be a caring person. It causes you to lie awake at night, praying and crying.

There was the little mother with six children who begged me to take at least one. Pushing a four-year-old toward me, she called attention to her beautiful hair and face, mentioning that she was the brightest of her children.

"Please take her, *Señora*," the mother pleaded. "I cannot feed them all." It was evident that she had prepared the child in advance. The little one smiled winsomely and reached for my hand. When I could not accede to the mother's request, both mother and child turned to go, weeping.

But not always did I have the resolve to say no. Sometimes my heart won, and our household enlarged. We seemed always to have several children besides our David, who loved having the others around. One time when George, returning from a trip, found an extra child I could not turn away, he "felt led" to put his foot down. Exhausted from the trip and longing for the comfort and quietness of home, he found me going in all directions to meet the needs of the clamorous household.

That night, after the children were asleep, George soberly informed me that our home could no longer be a refuge for neglected children. By giving more time and effort to the evangelization of the women, I would also help them bear the burden of their poverty and large families. I knew my husband was right. We would stop with the four we presently had.

But the next time, it was George who was unable to turn aside the pleas to help a needy child. He found Benedita on a trip to the mountains. She was 12, and her Christian parents had begged him to take her into his home in order to protect her from evil men in that area. Benedita was a lovely child with thick braids and beautiful dark eyes. Immediately I loved her.

The trip, George said, had been a frightening ex-

perience for the girl. She had never been away from
her remote mountain home. After four hours on the
trail by horseback, they arrived at the river, where a
raft floated them downstream to the road. There
they waited for a vehicle. When a truck loaded with
coffee beans came along, the passengers climbed
atop the sacks. Benedita clung to George in an agony
of fear. The railway—the next leg of the journey—
was worse. She screamed in terror as she saw the
noisy smoke-belching, bell-clanging locomotive. It
took George and two other men to get her aboard
the train, and it was some time before the frightened
child could relax. The trip concluded with a three-
hour ride on a rickety bus.

We put the exhausted girl to bed. The next morning Benedita awoke to a whole new world. She had
never seen an outdoor privy, much less a kerosene
stove or refrigerator, but she adjusted well to life in a
busy missionary household. She enjoyed the reading
lessons I gave her and was a great help in caring for
David.

With now five children in our home in addition to
David, I began to think of starting a school for our
believers' children. One day one of them came to us
in tears. Her school teacher had made her kneel on
hard grains of corn simply because she attended a
Protestant church. The teacher warned that the
punishment would be repeated if she returned to our
services. Many of the evangelicals preferred to have
their children illiterate than to endure such treatment.

I pressed George about the need, and he kept re-
minding me of mission policy. Clearly, there would
be no financial help from the mission if we started a

school. But the burden refused to go away, and the Holy Spirit continually drove me to my knees. George accused me of "nagging," and it was true! But for once it was my turn to suggest to him that God would have us "step out on faith." Finally, he agreed.

It was an exciting day when we told our believers if they would help build a school and stand with us in prayer and support, we would undertake to educate their children. We sent the same word to the congregations in the mountains. Although only a few could afford the pittance we were asking to cover food and a teacher's salary, we had the promise of 15 children.

Knowing that George could not neglect his district ministries, I faced the fact that the school would be largely my responsibility. Only the Spirit of God could have given us the courage to press on with such an impossible task. We had no money, no teacher, no backing. But we had the promise that "the one who is in you is greater than the one who is in the world" (1 John 4:4). We were poor, but for our people's sake we could be poorer in order that they might become rich in the knowledge of God's Word.

There was a large lot behind our house. For the honor and glory of God and for the preparation of future workers for His harvest field, there would be a school built upon it.

# *The New School*

THE POSSIBILITY OF AN EVANGELICAL school brought enthusiastic delegates from every area of our district. Since there was no money to buy materials, the men promised to cut bamboo and to bring it down the trail by mule-back—a difficult undertaking!

They tied bamboo poles six inches across and 20 feet long to the backs of mules, with the more slender part dragging behind. Not many could be carried at a time. The greatest problem was getting the poles around sharp curves and difficult places on the narrow trail. But so great was the desire of parents to see their children educated in an evangelical setting that they willingly made large sacrifices, taking many days from their work to cut and transport the materials.

The building's entire framework was of bamboo poles of varying widths. The walls were of split bamboo nailed to either side of the studding, then filled with mud. After the mud dried, the walls were plastered with a mixture of sand, cow manure and a little straw. This then received a thin coating of cow manure and sand, which, after it dried, was whitewashed.

One day while George was working with the men putting on the plaster, I became ill. I did not want to interrupt the work, so I said nothing. But the pain became so intense that I passed out on the floor of our porch. Our maid, excited and scared, ran to my husband, shouting, "Come, *Don Jorge*, the *Señora* just died!"

George came running, his hands still covered with the cow manure mixture. Grabbing a bucket of water, he began sloshing the water with his hands onto my face. I came to, aware of a pungent odor. When I realized that the smelly mess was all over me, I was irate!

Afterward we could laugh about it, but at the time I felt George might have at least taken time to wash his hands. But then, he had been told I was *dead!*

The school was planned to have a large open-air classroom with a boy's dormitory on one side and a teacher's room on the other. We were thankful that it was the dry season, for we had no money for the roof. Without a roof, the walls would disintegrate in the first rainstorm.

Our hope was to give the building a tile roof rather than thatch, for sanitary reasons, and we had been looking to the Lord for the money. Certainly neither the believers nor we had funds for such a purchase, and the people in North America did not know of our need. So we prayed for a miracle.

As the rainy season approached, George announced one morning that he was "stepping out on faith" for the tile. He was going to the local kiln to place his order. As the date drew near for the tiles to be ready, we were still without a peso to pay for them. Meanwhile, believers had brought lumber cut in the mountains, and George was busy making desks and blackboards. The desks were narrow tables, long enough to accommodate five students, with a shelf under the top for books. He also made benches.

The day we were to pick up the tiles, George went to the post office for the mail. He returned jubilantly waving a letter. In it was a check that provided the *exact* amount needed for the roof tiles! We were ecstatic. How we rejoiced to know that someone in the United States had been listening to the urge of God to send money to far off Gigante, Colombia. It was the miracle we needed to further assure us that our leading to provide a school was from the Lord. Our hearts were filled with praise to a God who delights in answering prayer and encouraging His children.

When the day came for the students to arrive, the fine Christian teacher we had contracted was ready and a woman in our congregation had offered to be the cook. A large new aluminum kettle, boiling Colombia's favorite soup, *sancocho*, was gradually turning black as it sat above the ground on three stones. A roof of thatch shaded the tables in our open-air dining room.

The poverty of the people permitted only a few to bring their things in a suitcase. The students came with bundles, boxes or their belongings tied in their blanket. The girls stayed in a large room next to our bedroom, and the boys slept in the dorm on bunk beds George had made. The accommodations were primitive, but they were as good as most had at home.

The first day of school was the fulfillment of our dreams. We stood before children ranging in age from 7 to 18. Some of the older boys were taller than I was, yet they did not know how to read. In faith we gave a New Testament to each one. The folding organ was a delight to the students as they learned gospel songs. Each day began with devotions.

Besides reading, writing and arithmetic, the children had social studies, Spanish grammar and Bible, and they learned the history and geography of Colombia. The school was in session six months of the year, leaving the remaining six months for me to travel with George in church planting. It was a joy to meet the educational needs of the evangelicals' children and to see God working in their lives.

We were to learn that there is much more to running a school in rural Colombia than housing, feeding and teaching the students. There came a day when George lined up every student and applied his head-lice concoction, tying each head in a cloth while it took effect. There was also a constant battle with bedbugs brought in with the clothing of the students, and cockroaches were something we learned to live with. In spite of DDT, the insecticide used at that time, the pests flew in from the neighbors' yards.

Our school was the main topic of conversation in the town. The priest's daily harangue against the evangelicals only increased the curiosity of the people. He said we were Communists and, therefore, haters of God. He promised excommunication to any who attended our church. He said our Bible was not the true Word of God but a false book. He cautioned that only priests could properly interpret it. Fearful Bible owners confessed to their sin of possessing the forbidden Book, and many of the confiscated Bibles were torched in the marketplace.

From his pulpit, the priest told the faithful that I

was a nun whom George had kidnapped from her convent and brought to Colombia. Our objective in starting a school, he said, was to teach children gross immoralities. I felt ashamed when I walked in town, knowing that most people would never doubt their priest. Our school children were likewise the object of this harassment, learning quickly that in following Christ there is a cross to bear. But we let them know that praying for those who persecuted them was an important part of Jesus' message.

One of our worst experiences was an epidemic of measles. Some of the children were very ill. I remembered my days at Nyack when I felt it imperative to study nursing as part of my training for missionary service. Now I wished I had more knowledge about caring for the sick. I did my best, though, to make each child as comfortable as possible.

It was at this time of extremity that the local doctor proved to be an angel in disguise. He prescribed medicine, he advised, he helped in many ways. More than that, he became our friend. It was a comfort to know he stood by us. We praised God that David's case was mild, for that gave us more time to help the others.

Measles was not the students' only affliction. At times it was necessary to treat ulcers caused by insects that deposit eggs under the skin. We gave medications for parasites and infections. One of the boys had an ulcer three inches wide, which I cleaned and treated several times a day for weeks, using sulfa drugs prescribed by the doctor. It was painful for him, and nothing seemed to help. But after a month of treatment, God answered prayer. Later that boy became a fervent preacher. I consider it a privilege to have knelt to cleanse his wound and encourage his heart.

Because of the Depression and reduced missionary salaries, we found it necessary to eat most of our meals out of the same kettle with the students. The thick *sancocho* made with yucca and plantain had but a square inch of meat per person. Rice and beans were always on the menu. Breakfast was bread and coffee or chocolate without milk. David loved it. After the students left for summer recess, he lamented that I did not cook as well as the *Señora*.

"The *Señora*"—Graciela—quite apart from meeting David's gastronomical desires, was an angel of light to us. Her husband drank heavily and would not support his family. She worked faithfully and without complaint under an open, grass-roofed shed through the heat of the day, cooking and serving the students with no better facilities than those three stones and soot-blackened kettles. Barefooted, her dark braid hanging against a patched dress, she would sing hymns as she toiled from morning to night. Graciela's sweet spirit and steadfast Christianity brought more blessing to my heart than a thousand sermons.

She had been just one more woman trapped in spiritual darkness until the day she timidly peeked in the door of our church. We invited her to stay, but the lies she had heard about us made her afraid. She kept returning, however, and one day she entered and sat down, her children squatting at her feet. To one whose life had been so devoid of love, the message of Jesus was good news indeed. She never missed a meeting after that.

Even when she was pregnant and about to deliver,

Graciela insisted on continuing her work as school cook. By then, conditions in her home on the outskirts of town were intolerable, and she and her children were occupying a small room behind the school. The room was anything but luxurious, but for Graciela it was like heaven to have a roof that did not leak and to know that her children would have food to eat.

When Graciela went into labor, I begged her to let me set up a bed in our house, but she insisted on staying in her room. I wanted to call the town doctor, but she would not hear of it. She asked only for newspapers to cover the dirt floor and clean rags.

Time after time during the night, I went to her door. She assured me she was all right, but she would not let me in. At last, exhausted, I fell asleep.

In the morning I hurried to her, only to find Graciela building a fire so she could cook breakfast for the students. Her smile was radiant and her joy was full. In a tiny hammock beside her was her new baby. What an example Graciela was to me whenever I was tempted to feel sorry for myself or to think my lot was difficult.

As the school year neared its close, we noticed a change in the attitude of the town people. Our students had uniforms: blue skirts and plaid blouses for the girls, blue shirts and dark pants for the boys. The students were impressive when we sometimes walked together through town at sundown. They could *read*—not as well as we desired, but they had learned how. Another six months of school would enable them to read well. There were evident positive changes in their lives, and all planned to return the next year.

The closing exercises were highly advertised by word of mouth. Many came to see what the evangelicals had done for their children and were amazed at all they had learned. The choir was especially impressive to them. By our standards the group would not have won a medal, but they sang with enthusiasm and genuine love for the Lord. Each student had also memorized many Scriptures. Their parents beamed with pride.

As we said good-bye to one another, there were many tears. We had lived together for six months, and we were sad to see them leave. Most of them came from areas too remote to attend our Gigante church, but their families were now a part of an evangelical community elsewhere.

The Gigante school had opened a door of ministry that before had been closed. Although we would never have more than 30 children at a time, we were preparing future students for our Bible school. One of our graduates would become president of the Colombian Christian and Missionary Alliance. One of the girls became the first president of the Women's Missionary Prayer Fellowship, serving effectively for many years. Others became pastors and pastors' wives. Many others were staunch, dedicated laypeople supporting their local churches.

How quiet it was after the last good-bye. That night, after David was asleep, I slipped out of the house to the open patio. There on a large stone beneath the tropical stars, I sat and reflected. I could see George inside, busy at the typewriter, oblivious to my absence, oblivious to the old loneliness I felt for family, friends and comforts in faraway Ohio.

It was a beautiful night. The stillness and the fra-

grance of honeysuckle stirred my being with long-
ings I thought I had conquered. Tears flowed and
sobs racked my body as I recalled loved ones and life
in Wadsworth. I did not realize how exhausted I was.
My romantic nature made me want my husband to
hold me in his arms. But he typed on and on.

Finally, about 11 o'clock, I watched him go from
room to room in search of me, then outside to
where — to his astonishment — I sat in tears. How different we were! He was so practical, so unmovable in
his nature and Christian life. I, by contrast, often
swung high and low.

That night as we sat beneath the stars so bright we
felt we could almost touch them, we expressed our
love for each other and our thankfulness for having
been brought together for God's work. We talked of
all that our homeland offered. But we had no desire
to turn back. We might sometimes get that ice-
cream-cone longing or want fellowship and fun with
other young couples, but we were genuinely glad we
were missionaries. We thanked God for the dear
Colombian friends we loved so sincerely. Their
heartaches, their poverty, their persecution were a
part of our lives. We were brothers and sisters in
Christ. By the power of the Holy Spirit we would be
faithful examples to them.

# *The Trail*

COLOMBIAN SMALL TOWNS ARE USUALLY built around a public square called *la plaza*. The church dominates this square, towering above the small shops surrounding it.

Gigante had a second mark of distinction—a giant Ceiba tree in the center of the plaza. Its lower branches were more than two feet thick. Beneath those spreading branches people set up open market early Monday mornings. Under its canopy business deals were made, town gossip was exchanged and, at noon, travelers observed siesta. Rumor had it that the town's name, meaning giant, had been inspired by the hugh tree.

On Sunday afternoons the road and trails into town were filled with people bringing produce to market. Sunday evenings the outside corridor of our house, where we held church services, was overcrowded, with people standing in the patio. A five-in-the-morning prayer meeting before Monday market fortified believers for the persecution they were certain to encounter.

Living in Gigante meant awaking each morning to the clang of church bells calling the people to early mass. The pealing bells, echoing across the valley and bouncing off the slopes of the Andes, also called us to morning devotions. Tolling bells and the song of tropical birds started our days with melody.

During school recess, David and I could accompany George on some of his trips. For trips that required a longer absence from home, we sometimes left David in the care of visiting missionaries.

On the trail we passed banana groves and thatched homes outside which naked children played in the sunshine. Colorful birds flitted through the trees. Flocks of parakeets, frightened from their resting place, winged away like a fluttering green scarf against the blue of the sky. Often we had to bend low over our animals to get through thick, overhanging branches and vines. George rode ahead, swinging his machete to clear the way.

Some trails led around the side of mountains and along the edges of precipices. It was not unusual for the horses to have to leap over rotting logs. Many times the rain pelted our rubber ponchos and hats as we sloshed along. The ponchos were large enough to cover us and the blankets tied behind us. At times the horses had to plow through mud almost to their knees. As they pulled out one hoof after the other, globs of mud fell in showers over us.

Once my horse slipped and fell, almost rolling on me. God's care and youthful agility saved me from disaster. Another time, as we rode along the side of a cliff, the strap of my saddle broke, and I found myself going over the horse's head. Frantically I clung to his mane. The horse knew he could not stop at that dangerous place. Panic changed to praise as we reached a place where I could dismount, and I felt solid earth beneath my feet. At such times I praised

God for giving me a rock-of-Gibraltar husband. His reassurance and help took me through many experiences I might not have survived alone.

Although there were steep mountains to climb, there were also beautiful valleys where many new-born babes in Christ waited with a good meal and a house overflowing with neighbors they had invited to hear the gospel. Even though there was singing before the sermon, the believers always begged for more afterward. Our folding organ, carried on a pack mule, supplied the music. Actually it was the only music they had, for this was before the day of transistor radios.

At one home, the only chair for me to sit on as I pumped the organ was of cowhide over a wood frame. The hide had stretched so badly that it formed a hole as deep as a washbasin into which I sank. I had to stretch my short legs to reach the pedals while the chair frame cut into the back of my knees. George had closed the service, but everyone begged for more singing so they would not forget the hymns. George was blessed with unlimited enthusiasm. After another hour of constant pumping, I whispered to George in English that I could *not* pump for even one more song.

Then they showed me my bed—the usual wooden frame without mattress, just a sheet on bare boards. I thought enviously of George, comfortable in his hammock in the open air. To make matters worse, several men came into the room to lie on cowhides on the floor. How could I sleep in that room with those men? I confronted George with the problem. He laughed! Traveling in the Andes would offer all kinds of unusual experiences that I would have to get used to.

By then some women had entered the room as well. Thus reassured, I returned to my bed. As they unrolled cowhides on the floor, I realized that as guest of honor I had been given the only bed. I was sorry I had complained.

Gradually it was wall-to-wall people in the room, most of them discussing the meeting that had just concluded. To make sleeping less possible, someone closed the only window, remarking that the night air was bad for people. Mothers nursed their babies. Men snored. Children cried. The room filled with the dank odor of sweating bodies and babies' urine. My body ached from the trip and the bed.

At four o'clock, everyone was up. Since we all slept in our clothes, we were ready for the day after a splash of water on our faces and a cup of thick, black coffee in our stomachs.

Nearly everywhere we went, there were people to be baptized. That meant several services, much singing and food-fests. In those days, people were not baptized until they had completed indoctrination classes and their personal lives had been thoroughly investigated. This, of course, required many trips. Many of the baptisms took place in mountain streams fed by snow caps. With 15 to 20 people to baptize, it was an ordeal for George to stand waist-deep in the bitter cold water. The people in those areas do not subject themselves to such torture, even to bathe, so it took great courage for them, as well. Not surprising, George often returned home with a severe cold after a baptismal service in icy waters.

George's ability to sleep anywhere had to be a gift

from God. He preferred to sleep outdoors on the wooden trays used for drying coffee or, in bad weather, in his hammock above the sleeping people in small rooms. He could sleep on bags of coffee or corn and on pressed sugar cane, called *bagazo*, using his saddle for a pillow.

One night, after traveling on horseback for hours, we had one of those long meetings when people did not want to quit. They offered us a small bed, but George spotted a loft where dried sugar cane was stored, and he asked for permission to spread our blankets there. Soon all was quiet and George was sound asleep. I could not sleep because of the cockroaches crawling all over us. In the beam of my flashlight I noticed that George's shirt pocket was black with the odious creatures. George slept on, now and then unconsciously brushing them from his face. Then I discovered that he had put a chunk of hard brown sugar in his shirt pocket, and that was what was attracting the cockroaches. I threw the sugar to the floor, but it was not a good night.

Few people returned to their homes after the evening service. Nearly all stayed overnight so they could hear another explanation of the Bible before going to work the next day. As we ate breakfast, we watched the dawn break over the rugged Andean peaks and marveled at the beauty of God's creation in those isolated regions. We were seeing grandeur that the wealthy of this world would never see because they would not accept the kind of accommodations we took for granted. Virgin forests climbed in dark green splendor to the snow caps. Small patches of farmland carved out of the mountainsides along the trails showed us how far our people had traveled to reach the meeting place.

Along the trail we stopped at many homes to leave literature and make new friends as we shared the gospel. The final hours of every trip were against the setting sun as we traversed the wide valley leading into Gigante. We arrived home with faces scarlet from sunburn, happy to clasp a beautiful little boy in our arms and feel the deep satisfaction of being God's missionaries.

As the time drew near for David's brother to put in his appearance, our intention was to cross the Andes, where we would have the services of an American doctor. But because of fatigue and the ruggedness of the trip, we decided to stay in Gigante. Our Colombian doctor delivered the baby in our home, and an English nurse from another mission came to assist us.

What a delightful addition to our household was our new little son! We named him George Wesley, but from the beginning we called him Joey. Even as a baby, he had a zest for living that won Colombian hearts. From the start, it was evident that he was going to do things his way, and he could charm everyone into accepting it.

We had been in Colombia five years. It was exciting to think about returning to our homeland, yet we felt reluctant to leave our dear Colombians. We had broken down many barriers and had made many friends in the town and province. People had become accustomed to an evangelical church in their town. Above all, the Christians' testimonies had made an impact. They had stood strong through ridicule and persecution. They carried their Bibles with pride. Homes had been changed for the better, abused children were loved and the Word of God had bound husbands and wives together.

Out on the small coffee farms, Christians sang as they picked coffee. At rest breaks, they read the Bible and discussed the truths of Scripture. At night they worshiped the Lord with vibrant singing and testimonies that drew many curious to listen. Many of the curious ones would not have accepted an invitation to an evangelical church service, but isolated on farms away from the scrutiny of priest and family, they came, they met the Lord and they were transformed.

## The Coffee Picker*

It's sunrise in the tropics,
  And morning's rosy glow
On the towering Andes,
  Topped with ice and snow,
Calls my heart to worship;
  I fall upon my knees
And ask God's help while picking
  Coffee from the trees.

And so I go each morning,
  Basket round my neck;
Nine long hours of picking
  Coffee peck by peck.
Once my job I hated,
  Now I work with ease
And happily pick coffee
  From the coffee trees.

Through the morning hours
   The coffee grove will ring
With the songs I'm singing
   To my Lord and King.
Other pickers listen
   (My message is to these)
While I pick the coffee
   From the coffee trees.

Once I was a sinner,
   Now I'm saved by grace;
Though I'm hot and weary,
   A smile is on my face.
Sometimes pickers listen,
   And sometimes pickers tease
While I'm picking coffee
   From the coffee trees.

When I've picked the coffee
   From the branches low,
I must climb a ladder
   To pick the top, I know.
Lord, will you protect me —
   Hold that ladder, please —
While I pick the coffee
   From the coffee trees.

Help me learn a lesson
   To reach up and to climb
For the fruit and blessing
   That, by faith, is mine.
In safety or in danger,
   In health or with disease,
To praise You while I'm picking
   Coffee from the trees.

Twelve o'clock! I'm hungry!
   This work makes one tire,

So I'll heat my coffee
  On my little fire.
I'll read God's Word and rest,
  My appetite appease,
And then I'll go on picking
  Coffee from the trees.

Coffee trees' white blossoms
  With their fragrance rare
Are beautiful to look at,
  Scenting all the air.
Yesterday, just blossoms,
  Now, plump berries, these—
I quickly fill my basket
  With coffee from the trees.

Coffee berries turning
  From dull green to red;
Ready now for harvest,
  Then to the oven fed.
Heat and grinding needed
  If the brew would please,
They need *me* for picking
  Coffee from the trees.

Some pick, some roast, some grind;
  Each one's helping hands
Do their part to send
  Coffee to all lands.
My wages let me send
  God's Word beyond the seas,
So happily I pick
  Coffee from the trees.

Shadows from the snowcaps
  And the setting sun
Declare our work is finished
  And the day is done.

I gave a tract and witnessed,
  I know my God I pleased,
While I picked the coffee
  From the coffee trees.

The first thing in the morning
  And the last at night—
A steaming cup of coffee
  Makes the day all right.
Every race of people,
  Aleuts or Sudanese,
Know about the coffee
  From the coffee trees.

Yet . . . Many still in darkness
  For the gospel wait,
But for me, the message
  Did not come too late.
So I'll give an off'ring,
  Pray much on my knees,
Witness while I'm picking
  Coffee from the trees.

Oh, I'm just a coffee picker,
  Nothing more am I.
I could not preach a sermon
  No matter how I'd try.
But I can let Christ's Spirit
  Blow love's gentle breeze
While I pick the coffee
  From the coffee trees.

And hearts with no desire
  For the truth to search,
Who will not read the Bible
  And will not go to church,
Will hear my testimony,
  My song upon the breeze,

While I pick the coffee
From the coffee trees.

Perhaps some day in heaven
When coffee picking's done,
No more baskets 'round my neck,
No tears, no burning sun,
No hands all stained and ugly
But clean and robed in white,
I'll greet my coffee-picking friends
In heaven's eternal light.

And, oh, I'd be so happy
If I could hear Christ say,
"Come, my coffee picker,
Come on home to stay.
You've been faithful daily,
Winning all of these
Who, with you, picked coffee
From the coffee trees."

But if only five or six
Enter heaven's door,
This coffee picker will rejoice
And sing forever more.
For I will be so happy
To know my Lord I pleased
While I picked the coffee
From the coffee trees.

Helen Constance

*This monologue is best appreciated by an audience if it is
memorized and acted out. Wear old clothes—an old blouse and
jeans, old shoes. Props needed:
  A tree, real or artificial, to stand beside
  A peck basket with rope to hang it around neck
  A step ladder to use when picking from top of tree
  A coffee mug

Stanza 2   Hang basket around neck; pretend to pick coffee beans from tree.

Stanza 5   Climb ladder; pretend to pick from top of tree.

Stanza 6   Gesture upward.

Stanza 7   Look at watch; descend from ladder.

Stanza 12   Pretend to drink "a steaming cup of coffee."

Stanza 16   At "no more baskets," remove basket from neck; show clean hands.

# *The Storm*

THE TROPICAL STORM PELTED the roof with sheets of rain. Lightning flashed against the blackness of the night, and deafening peals of thunder resounded over our adobe home. I could hear the rush of water as it coursed through gullies toward the river.

But it was not the storm that had me awake at three in the morning. It was my husband's absence — on what he chose to call an "exploratory trip" into the Amazon region of southeastern Colombia. I could still sense the shock I felt when George announced his intentions two weeks earlier. He wanted to make a month-long trip into the Amazon before our furlough. For some time, he said, he had been feeling that God was leading us to settle in that great unevangelized area when we returned to Colombia.

Not for a moment had it occurred to me that we would not return after our furlough to the mountain villages and towns of southern Colombia, where young churches needed us. Certainly with many towns as yet unevangelized, our work was not finished. I also wanted to carry on the work of the school, providing Christian education for the growing number of evangelical young people.

Most of all, I was a mother, and I feared for our two boys. Even in Gigante life was not easy. At least once a week we had to pick *niguas*—tiny fleas that burrow under toenails and lay eggs—from our boys' feet. This entailed pricking the flea sack and lifting out eggs and flea. It left their toes burning and itchy. Healing took days. The boys accepted this as part of life, and every Colombian country child went through the same ordeal.

Then there were the parasites. I could not forget my horror when I discovered a 10-inch live worm as I lifted my two-year-old from his potty-chair. I knew the protruding abdomens of so many children was due to parasites. But I had been careful about the food my children ate. The medicine to kill worms had unpleasant side effects.

Now George was intending that we take our boys beyond the reach of medical help to face the hazards of the vast Amazon jungle. To me it was unthinkable.

"Do you really believe that the Amazon, so isolated and primitive, is a place to take our boys?" I had protested.

George had not answered me directly. Instead, he asked, "Will you pray about it?" I would "pray about it," indeed, but I knew I was not willing to go to the Amazon!

All my efforts to dissuade George from making the trip had been fruitless. Once again He had sensed the call of God, and he intended to answer it. Lovingly he explained that he would never force me to go to the Amazon against my will. If God wanted us there, He would make it clear to both of us. In the meantime, he had to "spy out the land." And so, on a beautiful morning, he had kissed me good-bye as he and a national pastor set out to investigate Colombia's Amazon basin.

I wondered if the storm swirling around our Gigante house portended some dire calamity my absent husband was facing in the Amazon. It certainly expressed the turmoil of my heart.

A month from their departure, the two men returned on schedule. But George was barely recognizable. He had lost 20 pounds, and his complexion was the color of a pale orange.

The national pastor took me aside. "Ay, *Señora*, your husband almost died!" Then he told me how George had been stricken with malaria in the jungle. He had raged with fever they thought would never break. The pastor said his great fear was that they might have to bury my husband in the jungle. He covered his face with his hands. "How could I have returned to you, *Señora*, with such tidings!"

What gratitude I felt for that dear man who had cared for my husband during those weeks. Yet even as I expressed my thanks, I was conscious of a new fear in my heart. The pastor shook his head as he told me of the hardships of travel and living in the Amazon. He summarized his opinion by remarking that the jungle was "no place for *gringos*."

George was weak, but I detected no sign of discouragement as he talked of the possibilities for missionary work in that area. He told of villages of colonists trying to eke out a living from fishing while carving out small farms from government-donated land. There was one small Catholic school and mission, and Catholic priests went into the area monthly to say mass. Some evangelicals had traveled the

rivers, giving out tracts and selling Scriptures in settlements along the banks. But they no longer did so.

The village of Leguizamo (Le GHEE zah moh), on
the great Putumayo River, was where George wanted
to establish a mission. The Putumayo, one of the
tributaries of the Amazon, forms the boundaries for
Colombia, Ecuador and Peru.

As he talked, I studied George's thin face. Before
his illness he had had opportunity to do some
preaching in the Amazon. His eyes sparkled with
enthusiasm as he described the response of the people. I knew instinctively that, as far as George was
concerned, the issue was already settled. I was gazing
at another Apostle Paul saying "Christ's love compels
us." But what about George's promise that unless I,
too, felt God's call, we would not go? What about the
welfare of our two young sons?

"Continue to pray about it," was George's only response. *Continue to pray about it.* I promised him I
would, but in my heart the storm was still raging.

Adjustment to furlough in the United States was
more difficult than I had anticipated. I trembled behind the oversized pulpits whenever I was asked to
speak to church congregations. I was shocked by the
opulence of American homes. After five years
among some of the world's poorest people, I did not
feel at ease amid the sophisticated members of our
homeland churches. Ruefully I wondered how much
more we could have accomplished for Christ had a
little more of that wealth been available for needed
projects and equipment.

I had come from Colombia with shattered nerves
and two lively boys. George was away most of the
time on speaking engagements, leaving me with

most of the household responsibilities. I battled weakness and pain that had persisted for years. The medical examiner in New York advised that we stay home and get into another type of ministry. My husband was dismayed! He need not have been, for the missionary call of God on my life was more real than ever. It was strength that I lacked. We were grateful that our board granted us several extra months of rest beyond the normal one-year furlough. Meanwhile, God's people were praying.

As I looked at my strong husband, who was so anxious to get back to his work, I wished I had his stamina. My heart cried out to God that I not be a hindrance to a man of such deep concern for those lost without Christ. His entire makeup was that of a pioneer. His vigor would not be any easier to keep up with than it had been during the first term, but I was determined to keep pace as best I could.

Of course, there was still the unresolved issue of our sphere of work the next term. The Colombia missionaries had formally asked our homeland board for permission to open a base in the Amazon. While the months passed, I prayed that the board would not look favorably on this request. To my dismay, they granted permission for us to present this need to our churches and to receive offerings for it. I could feel the noose tightening. Especially when pressure lamps, air mattresses, a kerosene refrigerator and similar items needed for jungle living began to come in. Clearly, God was answering my husband's prayers, not mine. My fear of the unknown intensified.

One of the highlights for furloughing Christian and Missionary Alliance missionaries is the church's annual General Council. What joyful reunions we had with schoolmates who, like ourselves, were serving the Lord in every corner of North America and the world. How blessed, too, to meet people who had prayed faithfully for us as we represented them in Colombia.

Nevertheless, I was miserable. The Council missionary meetings and preaching services left me disturbed and guilt-ridden. I was willing to be God's missionary, but not in the Amazon. I loved the work of God, and my heart yearned over the lost, but my zeal stopped dead when I thought of having to bypass our former area of service and go to the jungle. I tried to be willing, but I knew God knew I was not. The storm still lashed a fury of doubt and fear within my soul.

One evening, conviction hung so heavy upon me that I felt I was being crushed. What if I gave in and God should take the life of George or one of the children in an area remote from other missionaries? Was it right to subject my children to the malaria that almost killed their father? As the invitation was extended, I realized those questions were not the issue. I had been *rebellious*, refusing the Holy Spirit's call to personal surrender. The issue was clear-cut: Was I willing to surrender my own life in obedience to the call of God?

As the last verse of the invitation hymn was being sung, I walked that long aisle, falling in a flood of tears at the altar. Saying yes to God was not in my own ability, but the Spirit of God so permeated my being that in an agony of grief and repentance, I yielded myself and my family to God's will.

That night, God exchanged my surrender for a

deep, settled peace. The storm was over. We would go to the Amazon.

America was in World War 2 as we arranged for our return. We managed to get aboard a ship leaving from New Orleans for Panama. After a month in San Cristobal, we got passage on a small launch bound for Cartagena. The vessel was far overloaded and indescribably filthy. To make matters worse, we hit a raging storm the second night out that tossed us against the walls of our tiny cabin. It was a distinct relief when we finally put our feet on solid Colombian soil.

Five days and six nights on a Magdalena sternwheeler took us through the heart of Colombia. Two days of train travel and a three-hour ride on a rickety bus brought us once again to Gigante.

What a reunion! Fred and Della Smith, the missionaries who had taken our place, told us how the work had grown. Believers converted under our ministry welcomed us back. That night we stood in our favorite spot beside the trees near the cliff. Below us the murmuring water splashed over rocks on its way downstream. Standing beneath the bright stars, we remembered how God had promised Abraham offspring as uncountable as the stars. We praised God for the fruitful work of our colleagues. Though we would be leaving the area we had come to love, we were confident the ministry would continue to expand.

Within a month George was off to the jungle to find a place for us to live. It was a glad day when he returned, this time healthy and enthusiastic about our new venture. He had found a sizable house under construction in Leguizamo, and the builder—

a woman—was willing to rent it to us. It would be of rough boards, crude by American standards, but it would be ours when it was ready.

While we waited, we visited the rural churches, rejoicing to see for ourselves the way the gospel was penetrating these mountain regions. We also announced a convention for all the churches in the area. Knowing it would be the last one that we would be leading, everyone planned to attend. We wondered how we could accommodate them all. Dear Graciela was on hand as the cook, and we knew that the appetizing meals would be ready on time. We also knew that Graciela's winsome smile and willing spirit would add much to the success of the convention.

The people overflowed the wooden benches and the available floor space. Many stood in the yard. They slept on the benches, on the ground and wherever they could find space for their cowhide mats. Testimony time thrilled us as they told of their battles, their victories and of the reality of Christ in their hearts. Out of their poverty they brought generous offerings to help support Colombian pastors.

It was hard to say good-bye, but it was time to leave for our new work in the Amazon. As we loaded the truck, our friends gathered to wish us well and to give their gifts of love—fruit, flowers and sweets. We all wept as we parted.

Behind us, the old adobe house, the river's song, the wide valley, the mighty mountain and the orchid-filled tree would be a beautiful picture in our minds forever. Ahead, only God knew what awaited us as we set our faces toward the Amazon jungle of eastern Colombia.

# The Jungle

THE OLD TRUCK, LOADED WITH OUR possessions, stopped in front of a rooming house in Florencia, the last town before the jungle. At Florencia the road ended. From there on, the Ortaguasa River was the only means of surface travel.

It was the dry season, and the road over the Eastern Cordillera had provided its own adventure of faith. Each time we passed an approaching vehicle, we could see nothing until we came through the dust cloud, and by that time we were rounding one of the innumerable hairpin curves.

We alighted from our precarious seats totally dust covered. Our hair was stiff with powdered earth, and our clothes were brown, no matter what their original color had been.

The next three days were filled with preparations for the river trip. We were counting on buying fruit and plantain from Indian settlements along the way, but George bought great chunks of meat, which we cut into thin strips and salted. These he hung to dry on a pole in the sun. That dried meat would be the basis for our meals. George bought bags of rice, beans, lentils and onions, which he stacked in a corner of our room. The day before we left, I filled containers with boiled water.

I could hardly believe the size of the dugout George had bought. It was 30 feet long, carved by Indians out of a single cedar log. Originally it was pointed at either end, like a canoe, but George had sawed off and boarded up one end to accommodate the outboard motor. There were two slatted benches for the boys and I to sit on. A hired boatman would sit on the prow to push away floating logs and help steer. George would handle the motor.

As I looked at the river and that frail craft, my old fears for my children returned. It had been much easier to yield my life to Christ in an inspirational meeting in the United States than it was to live out that commitment on the edge of the jungle. But we were at the point of no return; I had no option but to go forward.

At dawn the next morning we loaded the canoe. Curious people joined the cluster of Christians gathered to see us off. Together we prayed to God for protection on the journey.

The canoe was so ladened that only a few inches remained above water. Seated on the short-legged bench with one arm around David and the other around Joey, I waited for George to pull the starter cord. Two yanks and we were off, leaving the waving people and the last town behind. Ahead of us were no motels, no supply stations, no friends in time of need. This time we really were stepping out on faith, and I was not quite sure God could answer our prayers without some civilization around.

As the last of the huts on the edge of Florencia disappeared from view, we began to enjoy the beauty of the early morning. The forest was a lush green and the sky a deep blue dotted with puffs of fleecy clouds. The river itself was a ribbon of crystal water winding ahead of us into the unknown. Slowly the tension drained from my body. The boys delighted in splashing their hands in the water.

Soon, as we rounded a curve, the boys discovered they could play in water *inside* the canoe. The spray soaked our clothes, and we laughed at the coolness as the wind dried them. We were glad for slatted platforms across the rounded bottom of the canoe to keep our supplies from getting wet. We were glad also that the water could slosh below the racks without touching our feet. Otherwise, it would have been a long foot bath! We kept bailing out water all along the way.

The morning hours were delightful. But as the noonday sun began to burn our skin, George beached the craft in shade while he looked for small saplings he could bend to support a canvas canopy over us. George's helmet protected him somewhat from the sun, and he used it to scoop water over his body, clothes and all.

For the boys, the trip was sheer delight. They played around the canoe, climbing over benches and baggage, dabbling in the water and watching the flying fish. For naps we had prepared a spot atop the baggage. As for me, I had my supply of books and magazines—damp with spray. But the scenery was too fascinating and my boys were too active for much reading.

As we passed small islands, the noise of our motor stirred flights of white egrets. At other times, when the current took us close to shore, a streak of green parrots winged away into the forest.

In the tropics, there is a very short twilight. So around four in the afternoon, we began to watch for a suitable place to camp. Since it was dry season, great sandbars lined the curves of the river. We had hoped for an Indian shelter, but not finding one, George shouted above the noise of the motor that we would sleep on the sand. As he started to draw near one of the lovely beaches, 8 or 10 sleeping crocodiles aroused themselves and slithered into the water. Frantically I signaled George to go on. After we had passed three more beaches similarly populated—and with similar reactions from me—George simply pulled onto the next sandbar with such speed that he beached the craft before the reptiles had completely disappeared in the water.

The boatman gathered wood for a fire, and we prepared rice and beans for supper while the boys raced up and down the beach, glad to run free. As darkness fell, we seemed very small out there in all that immensity. Visions of those crocodile jaws made washing dishes at the river's edge a bit unnerving, but they did not reappear. Swarms of mosquitoes were less timid. They hissed around our heads, undeterred by repellant.

Convinced by our boatman that all living things would leave the area if he hit the water with his paddle, we let him pound while we bathed the boys and enjoyed a short but refreshing nocturnal swim. Had I not insisted that we bypass the first several sandbars, we could have done all that in daylight.

It had been a long day. We laid our blankets by the fire, with the boys between us. Exhausted from the heat and strain, George fell asleep immediately. David and Joey talked about the wonders of the day, but soon they, too, slept. Somehow the sand that had looked so soft felt like cement under me. In spite of my weariness, I could not sleep. I marveled at how low the stars hung over the silent river. Every now and then a great fish flapped its tail in the water. In the darkness of the night, it was frightening. I felt prompted to refuel our dying fire in hopes of keeping away the jaguars that roamed the nearby forest. At last, just as the flickering light of dawn began to show, I fell asleep.

It was nothing less than exasperating to see the enthusiasm with which my husband greeted the new day! He beat on his chest and loudly exclaimed about the beauty of the morning. My aching body and heavy eyelids regretted that the day had to start at all.

The boys awoke as enthusiastic as their dad. They ran the beach, hunting shells. The boatman had the fire going with plantains roasting and coffee boiling. A cup of the brew improved my attitude wonderfully. A short devotional encouraged us to trust God for another day on the river.

Following the channel was necessary when the waters were low. We often swung from one side to the other with the erratic current. The boatman saw to it that we were informed of the river's hazards: schools of red-bellied piranha that could clean the flesh from the bones of a man or animal in just a few minutes, the electric eel that carries enough current to electrocute a horse, the great anaconda whose 30-foot skins we had seen for sale in the cities, stingrays whose barbed tails can make the bravest man roll in agony. Yet he was sure that as long as he hit the water with his paddle, nothing would harm us.

Sometimes we passed the remains of Indian villages — skeletons of thatched homes on stilts. Yellow fever and measles had decimated the Indian population — something eliminated in more recent years by the introduction of modern medical procedures.

Most nights we slept on the beaches, but one afternoon we found an abandoned Indian hut, which we decided to take advantage of. After an early supper and a swim, we got settled before darkness fell. We lined the inside of each hammock with sheets, hoping the mosquitoes would not bite through them. With mosquito nets over us and walls around us, we felt secure. It was comforting to know that the notched log to our stilted hut would be difficult for animals to climb.

We were all sleeping peacefully when both children suddenly began to cry. By our flashlights we could see that they were covered with bites, as were we. The place was infested with bedbugs brought in by the transient Indians. The insects had climbed down the hammock ropes and swarmed all over us. We used repellant and lotions and finally George and David slept. But Joey, only three and a half, was so miserable that I climbed down the notched log with him. On the narrow beach there was a large log. Hesitantly I kicked it, half expecting it to move. It did not, so I sat down on it, covered Joey with a sheet to shield him from the mosquitoes, and gently rocked him. The beauty of the night fascinated me. From the forest behind me came the most unusual birdcalls. One close by called to its mate, whose answer from afar came floating back across the jungle. Back and forth the night birds called, while monkeys and other animals chimed in with a cacophony of shrieks, shrills, laughs, moans and screams.

As Joey slept, my tears fell on his curly head. My deepest fear was not of the things lurking in the darkness (though I feared them, too), but for the possibility of malaria or bedbug fever that might hurt my loved ones. For a long time I prayed and cried. Then a great relief swept over me and peace filled my heart. Just as the night bird received an answer from its mate, so God had heard my cry and sent His answer floating on the jungle breeze to my heart. *God was there with me!* The memory of that night has been a priceless treasure.

I knew that most people would consider us foolish to have let ourselves into such a situation as this. In the natural, it would have been foolish. But in God's planning, He had led us and was proving again that He meant it when He said, "Surely I will be with you always."

# CHAPTER
## 12

# *Leguizamo*

WE WERE ALMOST HOME—IF SUCH a cherished word dared to be used to describe a place three of us had never been. We had traveled eight days on the Ortaguasa and Caqueta Rivers to the jungle town of La Tagua, then by truck across a six-mile stretch of potholes and ruts to Leguizamo, on the bank of the Putumayo River. As we bumped along the dirt road into town, we could hardly wait to get a glimpse of our new house.

At last, there it was, more or less as we had mentally pictured it. Its shingled roof stood out against the sea of grass roofs surrounding it. As George had said, the house was made of rough-cut, unpainted boards. It had neither plaster nor insulation. We went from room to room, assessing its potential. There was a living room, a small dining room, a kitchen and three small bedrooms. The bathroom was an outhouse. What a challenge it would be to make this truly a home!

The ceilings were only boards laid across the rafters and nailed at each end. We were soon to discover that Leguizamo—and all the jungle area—was infested with rats. We had had rats in Gigante, but in the jungle the rats came in droves. We never saw them in the daytime, but at night those loose boards overhead sounded like percussion drums as the rats ran to and fro.

We did everything possible to battle the rats. We put rat poison in every place inaccessible to children. But with such multitudes, the death of a few rats meant nothing. We consulted the local citizens, who suggested a cat and even provided us with one. The rats ran the cat off.

The rats loved leather. We once left the house unattended for a week and returned to find the leather seat of a dining room chair entirely eaten. We had to keep our leather suitcases under the bed so we could protect them in the night if we heard gnawing. Rats transformed a pair of George's heavy boots into oxfords.

One of George's early-on projects was to position two metal drums to catch rainwater from the roof. This water he piped to a shower enclosure behind the house. During the dry season, we hired boys to carry water from the river.

The river was the town's major source of water, both for washing clothes and for bathing. In fact, the town went en masse to the river each day to bathe. The women wore loose muumuu-type dresses under whose ample folds they could modestly don bathing attire right on the beach. At first I declared I would not chance an encounter with the creatures I knew existed in that river. But when the heat became unbearable, I joined the crowd. Actually, it was one of the highlights of life in Leguizamo.

Three weeks after our arrival, my feet broke out in a rash I thought was athlete's foot. Day after day I applied a recommended salve, but the rash only spread. The burning and itching were intense. Then my feet began to swell. Finally, I could not walk. I was anxious to get on with our work in Leguizamo; instead, I was helpless!

George was getting acquainted in the town, and he brought people to the house to meet me. Each one suggested his or her own special remedy for my trouble, assuring me of relief. The medication for athlete's foot was ineffective, so I was ready for alternatives. But nothing worked! The enforced inactivity depressed me.

Many of my visitors said they had experienced similar problems when they first arrived in the jungle — they referred to it as "jungle rot." It was less than comforting to learn that it usually took from six to eight weeks to run its course and that some never did fully recover. One woman cited her sister's case: the condition became so advanced that both legs had to be amputated.

Motivated by such counsel, I sought divine healing with renewed resolve. I reminded the Lord that His work was at stake. We were at the end of our resources. The only pharmacist in town had run out of suggestions. God's Word became my consolation, and I learned more about prayer during those weeks of enforced rest than at any other time.

One day, I noticed the oozing rash was beginning to dry. Hope filled my heart. Sure enough! The condition gradually subsided, and I never suffered from it again. God had done what no remedy could.

Leguizamo was typical of the Amazon frontier towns of that era. The thatch houses were typical. The unpaved streets all ending at the river were typical. But Leguizamo was strategic. Crossing the Putumayo put us in Peru. If we traveled 60 miles west by river, we could be in Ecuador. All aspects of life in that region depended on the river. There was no other means of surface travel. Riverboats brought staples such as rice, beans, lentils, chickpeas and sometimes cabbage. For most of the populace, the river was not only highway but laundry room, larder, bathroom and playground.

The town's population comprised five groups of people: Indians who had left their tribal areas deeper in the jungle, colonizers lured by the offer of free government land, a few merchants weary of city life, civilians working at the mini naval base and fugitives from the law.

Few frontier towns are models of moral probity, and Leguizamo was no exception. We soon discovered that one of the town's brothels was next door to us. Several of the girls were obviously Indians, and some looked not more than 12 years old. Our hearts were grieved at their plight. Drunken sailors often beat them mercilessly before the nights were over. Many times I stood at my window in the darkness unable to sleep because of the loud music and the commotion next door.

Many of the thatch huts were occupied by women who had been abandoned by the sailors who fathered their children. With no means of livelihood except to wash clothes in the river, they found it easier to be common-law wives to sailors assigned to the local base. Theirs was a sad life — forever being promised marriage and security, only to be abandoned once and again. The extreme poverty in some of these single-parent households prompted mothers to give their 11-year-old daughters to the sailors. Our

hearts were saddened by the ravages of sin all around
us. Surely Leguizamo offered a golden opportunity
for grace to abound.

The arrival of Protestant missionaries from North
America caused quite a stir in the town, especially
when we began at once to reach out in love and
concern to the people. Right across the street from
our house was a building suitable for meetings. This
we were able to buy. The people whom George had
met during his two exploratory trips were the first to
respond to our invitation of Sunday services. Music
and curiosity brought others. Soon we had a small
congregation and a Sunday school.

By virtue of a concordat between the Colombia
government and the Vatican, the Roman Catholic
Church had a complete monopoly of education in
what was then known as "Mission Territories," includ-
ing Leguizamo. The fact was that the church had
never established a school in Leguizamo. The ma-
laria-infested town with its isolation and poverty held
no attraction for the church beyond sending priests
once a month to hold a mass, baptize babies, collect
offerings and marry the rare couple who elected to
formally marry.

Recalling how our school in Gigante had been
used of God to open hearts and homes to the gospel
and to greatly expand the church, we decided to
trust God for a similar experience in Leguizamo.

As in Gigante, George began making desks, black-
board and equipment for the school. Soon our
chapel was ready to double as a school during the
week. God helped us find a qualified teacher, and we
set a date to begin.

Before school opened, we had a session with the

parents, explaining our evangelical beliefs and the school's curriculum. We invited them to attend one of our church services so they would know better what to expect. Most of them had never been in a Protestant service, but they were impressed.

School opened with our students in uniform. We were proud of the children entrusted to our care. Actually, David was one of the students that first year. He learned to read Spanish before English. Joey was not old enough to be in school, but he was always there anyhow. It was a joy to supervise recess and see my boys participating in the fun. Every boy had a top—the kind that are spun with a string—and our boys were as proficient as any with their tops.

For special celebrations, we would load the big dugout with students, food and cooking utensils and head upriver to a sandbar for a day of games and fun. Returning home before sunset, the boatload of children filled the air with song that wafted over the town. We never considered how risky it might be to have 25 kids at a time in a dugout. We only knew they were the happiest kids in town.

Except for outings like that or special programs where George was involved, the national teacher and I carried the responsibility of the school. This left George free to travel during the week to evangelize other towns and villages.

We scheduled special programs so parents could see how much their children were learning. One of their impressive accomplishments was Bible memorization from the New Testaments each one had been given. Their singing ability made our programs the talk of the town.

Early in November we began preparing for our

Christmas Eve program. Beautiful Christmas poems and songs were available in Spanish, and the children vied with each other to memorize the longest ones. Every child was given a part. While we practiced, George was visiting along the river, advertising the program.

On Christmas Eve the river was lined with canoes. It was amusing to hear people complain that they had to tie their boats far upstream because there were no parking places near the town. That night, people packed the aisles of our chapel, sat on the floor and hung in the windows. Behind curtains we maneuvered students on and off stage and wiped perspiration from our brows.

As in Gigante, the angel choir of dusky-skinned children in white robes and tinsel halos stole the show. The three Wise Men were a bit off key, but their elaborate outfits made up for it. Near the end of the program, we announced treats for all in attendance. We knew that would hold the audience through George's 15-minute sermon explaining why Christ came to earth. Several responded to his invitation. Many bought Bibles at our subsidized price. The candy treat we distributed would be the only Christmas gift many received.

We dropped into bed that night utterly exhausted, knowing that at six in the morning the believers would be ready to leave for the promised Christmas Day celebration on the sand. It was a fun day for the boys. They enjoyed the water fights and swimming with the other children. They had no time to miss the traditional Christmas dinner that is such a part of North American Christmases. A leg of chicken and rice and beans were just fine as far as they were concerned.

As it is around the world in evangelical circles, baptisms are a highlight. Our Christmas with the Leguizamo believers on the Putumayo sandbar was such an occasion. It was thrilling to see these new believers emerge from the water with radiant faces. Their testimonies crowned the day and bathed our souls with joy.

As we returned home together in the big dugout, our children around us, we sang Christmas carols all the way. This, I suddenly realized, was the jungle I had once dreaded. Not in my whole life had I been so happy!

# 13

# *The Bitter Year*

L IFE, WE ALL KNOW, IS WHAT we make of it. But I was not always able to react in trusting faith when disappointments and other setbacks befell us. Our second year in the jungle seemed to have more than its share of such discouragements.

The time was approaching for David to enter our mission's school in Quito, Ecuador. The Alliance Academy was a generous provision. Quito is on the equator, but it is 9,000 feet above sea level — well above the malaria line — and the climate is invigorating and healthful.

Quito's healthful climate made us a little more willing to say good-bye to our eight-year-old for the long months of a school term. Not that David was experiencing physical problems. But it did seem that the jungle climate was taking its toll on him. One day a doctor, who had flown in to the naval base, passed our house and saw David playing.

"Your son needs to get out of this climate," the doctor commented to me. "He is pale and yellow. A cooler climate would greatly benefit him." Advice like that made it a little easier to send David off.

It was not possible for civilians to get passage on the small planes that serviced the military bases. The planes were always overloaded with military personnel. So, with suitcase lovingly packed with warmer clothing from our outfit, David and his father boarded one of the horrible river boats on the first leg of the long journey from Leguizamo, Colombia, to Quito, Ecuador.

I watched my boy leave, knowing he would not be home for nine months. That is a long time for an eight-year-old to be without his parents. We waved until the boat disappeared around the curve of the river. Then Joey and I walked back to the empty house. There on the bedroom floor, David's cast-off shorts lay crumpled. Joey's happy heart could go on enjoying life, but I fell to my knees in a flood of tears as I felt the first truly big sacrifice of my life. How small the problem of mosquitos, isolation, heat and the other things I had complained about! Separation from one of my children was a true test of my consecration to Christ and His will.

We had dedicated our sons to the Lord with the knowledge that one day they would leave for school in Ecuador. We had been sincere in our willingness for a sacrifice that we knew would require the grace of God. But as I endured the loneliness and the day-by-day yearning for a beloved son, the price seemed too great. The daytime hours were crowded with activity, leaving little time for reflection, but each evening as I watched the sun slip behind the vast jungle, my tears fell as I worried about the wretched food on the river boat, the long ride over the mountains and the final plane trip to Quito.

After two weeks, I assumed David and his father had arrived at the school. I envisioned my boy happily involved in studies, making new friends, exploring a new environment. The ache was there, especially when I put Joey to bed. It hurt to know someone else was taking my place, though I was thankful for the kindness of whomever that was.

One day we heard a boat's deep horn. I joined the rest of the town at river's edge. A boat meant things to buy and people to greet. To my joy, there was George, the only *gringo* aboard, swinging bags of provisions he had bought in the interior. How happy we were to see him! How eager I was to learn how David had fared!

I was totally unprepared for what George had to tell me. I learned that a radiogram had been sent to the military base in Leguizamo, which we had never received. The radiogram was intended to inform us that due to new construction at the school, classes would open in January, not August. George and David had arrived only to discover that they need not have gone until five months later.

I was devastated!

To have made the long trip back home, then within a couple of months to do it all over again, was not reasonable. Moreover, as we often experienced, in our extremity the Lord had a solution. Bob and Wilda Savage, missionaries with HCJB Radio in Quito, lovingly opened their hearts and home to our David. Their oldest child was nearly David's age. George assured me the two were having great times together.

I should have been grateful for this provision for David, and I was. I should have reasoned that a sovereign God, who has power to see that radiograms are delivered, may have purposely intervened to spare David debilitating sickness or even death had he remained another five months in the Amazon. Instead, I was angry—so angry I had no peace for days. And when I was not angry, I was full of self-pity. I wanted my little boy there to love. I wept as I thought of how David must feel—being sent away from home. Would he cry at night, wondering why he could not be with his family?

At night, while the rest of the family slept, Satan tormented me with his barbs. I felt I could have had victory if David were in school. But for my boy to have to spend five unnecessary months away from his family was a circumstance I could not accept. A "root of bitterness" made me miserable until I finally took my broken heart to Jesus and trusted Him to heal it. Letters from the Savages were balm to my soul. They assured us all was well.

Christmastime was especially hard. It was David's first Christmas away from home. We knew he would have a beautiful Christmas, but it hurt not to see his joy in opening gifts or to join in his fun. We prayed David would understand why he had to be away from us. We prayed he would know how much we loved him.

The second crushing blow came as our second year of elementary school drew toward a close. The year had begun with 60 students—a 50 percent increase. We were thrilled that those from the first year could read and write and were able to advance rapidly in their studies. All but one of the six girls living in the house with us were teenagers. We could not help but reflect how different their lives would be if the gospel had not gone to Leguizamo. We joined in their fun with volleyball, Ping-Pong and swimming. Older students witnessed to the town

people and younger ones read the Bible to their illiterate parents. Our Sunday services were crowded to
capacity. We were thrilled by the many answers to
prayer. People were signing up their children for the
next school year, and we were looking to God for
direction to accommodate them.

We were preparing for closing exercises when a
cable arrived from the Minister of Education. It instructed us to permanently close our school upon
termination of the current school year.

We were shocked!

It was hard to believe that a jungle area that had
been ignored for centuries should suddenly became
the concern of the Catholic hierarchy and the Minister of Education. Through the years, no one had
cared that children grew to adulthood illiterate and
doomed to a life of hopeless poverty. But now that
Protestant missionaries had subjected themselves to
the privation, heat and disease of the jungle, Leguizamo was important. Now that 60 happy children
were receiving intellectual, physical and spiritual
preparation for life, something would have to be
done about this threat to the church.

As we looked at the children and thought of the
200 applications for the next year, our hearts ached
with disappointment. As soon as possible, George
made a trip to Bogota to talk with the Minister of
Education. The minister was adamant. Not even the
sheaf of petitions from the people of Leguizamo
moved him. Catholic nuns would arrive within a
month to begin an elementary school in Leguizamo.

It was Gigante revisited. There was a perceptible
shift in people's attitude toward us. Attendance at
the chapel fell off. One morning I watched as two

nuns came down the street with a group of children. They were singing a song against Protestants that we had heard many times before. As they drew near, I peeked from the doorway. They stopped directly in front of our house, and the nuns told the children to begin throwing trash at our house. Some did so reluctantly.

I could not help it; my tears flowed and uncontrollable sobs shook my body. The harassment, the lies, the forced alienation of warm friends left me in despair. The Bible talked about "those who sow in tears" reaping "with songs of joy" (Psalm 126:5). We had wept as we sowed the seed, but somehow I could not find my song of joy. Our dream of an evangelical school in the jungle where hundreds of children would learn the truth had been shattered by fanatics who dared not let the Bible get into the hands of the people.

Indomitable George! An Ecuadoran family informed him that government land was available to us if we would start a school on the Ecuadoran side of the river. This would be a location about 60 miles west of Leguizamo. Immediately George set about to put such a school together. He secured the necessary permissions, selected a site and recruited Solomon and Chinca Manchola to head the operation. Solomon Manchola had been a student in our school in Gigante. He went on to graduate from Bible school. Later he would be a president of the Colombian Alliance Church. He brought his bride to the jungle, and with remarkable devotion and self-sacrifice they together founded a school and church that has impacted the Amazon. Special meetings in that far-off jungle post brought people from up and down the Putumayo River. George and I counted it a privilege to minister with Solomon and Chinca Manchola.

It was the new school in the Ecuador Amazon that helped account for our third crisis of the year. All during the summer I had been suffering with severe, intermittent pain in my right side. I feared appendicitis. I sought divine healing, but relief did not come. As the time neared for David to make his trip back to school, we decided I would make the trip instead of George. I would take David to where he could get a plane to Quito, then I would proceed on to the clinic of the Gospel Missionary Union for surgery. This would permit George to work unhindered on the new jungle school. I would take Joey as well, so George would have no family responsibilities. At the time, it sounded like a good idea.

George helped us hang our hammocks above the freight on the river boat. Then he kissed us each good-bye and set off for his own trip into the jungle. We knew there would be no way to get in touch with him for the next two months, but we had peace about it.

The boat trip was worse that I remembered. The filth, the terrible food, the lack of privacy, the squawking chickens, the heat all mingled fiendishly to make my days miserable. The barge was so loaded that to get to the toilet we had to cling to the *outside* of the rail, putting our feet between bars around the deck and hanging over the water as we clung to the rail.

The worst part of the trip was when the boat stopped to take on firewood for the stove or to buy provisions. This it did three or four times a night.

The yelling, the slamming of wood on deck, the cursing, the dickering for supplies, the drinking and fighting made sleep impossible for me. I was thankful when we arrived at Florencia.

The next day we crossed the Andes on one of the same dilapidated buses we had ridden years before. Nothing had changed. The hairpin curves brought on the same motion sickness. And when we went from bus to train, we had the same black soot I remembered from before.

We arrived in Popayan where David, accompanied by a Quito-bound missionary, flew on to school. It was easier to say good-bye this time because he was going back to friends and teachers he loved.

Leaving Joey in the care of missionaries at the Bible Institute, I set out alone for the GMU Clinic at Palmira. Not until I was traveling alone did I realize how really tired I was.

It was five in the afternoon when I arrived at the clinic. The doctor was ready to leave for the weekend, but after examining me, he decided to operate at once. I told him I had been traveling, but there was no way he could know how utterly exhausting the trip had been. It was a relief just to lie on the operating table and commit myself into the hands of the doctor and the Great Physician.

What followed I learned much later from the clinic nurse and the doctor. With the first whiff of ether, the anesthetic used at that time, I went into cardiac arrest. Frantically, the doctor worked to bring me around. Three times during the operation this happened, and each time the doctor worked desperately to save my life.

The doctor's weekend plans could not be altered,

so later that night he put me in the hands of his capable nurse and left town. That night my heart stopped three more times. The frantic missionary in charge of the clinic was going around asking, "Where in the world is this woman's husband?" I could only respond weakly that he was somewhere in the Amazon jungle.

Because the doctor had had to stop his surgery while he worked on my heart, infection had opportunity to enter the incision. For a month I lay weak and critically ill, my body fevered, my nervous system shattered, my mind depressed. I appreciated the Alliance nurse sent to give me full-time care while I was so sick. I appreciated the nurses and other personnel at the clinic who were so wonderful to me.

In my weakened state, I dreaded the thought of the long trip to Bogota where I would seek a seat on a military seaplane to Leguizamo. I wondered how long I would have to wait. If ever I needed the circle of my husband's strong arms, it was right then. A dark cloud settled over my soul when I realized that I did not want to go back to the jungle — *ever*. Despair filled my heart as I thought of the heat, the privation, the Satanic forces to be faced. I only wanted a place to hide, a place where I could be quiet. The thought of all the work at the end of the line made me sure I did not want to go back.

In the end, I had to face the fact that the jungle was the only home I had. Although I was still not well, Joey and I made the eight-hour train trip to Bogota, where kind friends gave us lodging while we waited for room on a flight.

At last the day came. As the plane splashed to a stop on the river at Leguizamo, I saw George waiting, and new hope filled my heart. How wonderful it was to be secure again with my husband! Until I told him, he had no idea of all that had happened during our weeks of separation. George lifted responsibility from my shoulders, and the sweet rest in my own home began to bring healing and a new enthusiasm for life and my call to God's work. Slowly the nerves healed and joy in God's service returned.

I realized that many of God's people in the homeland had been burdened for George and Helen Constance during those trying weeks. I was thankful for their faithful prayers!

# CHAPTER
## 14

# *Sylvia*

JOEY WAS SIX YEARS OLD, and the time was drawing near when he, too, would have to leave for school. Joey, with his blond, curly hair and winning smile, was a favorite in the town. Everyone loved him. His vigor and enthusiasm for marbles, top spinning and swimming kept kids coming in spite of the nuns' warnings to stay away from the Protestants. I wondered how I would ever live without the lively little boy who so captivated everyone's heart.

I could not bear the thought of having no children at home, and so we began to ask the Lord for another. When we knew a baby brother or sister was on the way, we were delighted.

Since there was no doctor in town, we made plans to exchange places with a Colombian pastor living in the city of Manizales. He and his wife were willing to take up ministry in the jungle, and we could live in their home in the city until after the baby's birth. For both families it would be an extreme change.

Our only hope of leaving the jungle by plane was the naval base, whose amphibian aircraft usually had no room for civilians. But, knowing of my pregnancy, the officials kindly consented to take us. As usual, the one-engine plane was overloaded, and the trip was scary. Crossing the interminable jungle, its sea of green broken only by a winding river below, we realized that if the plane should fall, we could be lost from view forever.

For the most part, the pilot followed the course of the river, barely skimming the tree tops. We sat behind him on the baggage along with several sick sailors who repeatedly crossed themselves and prayed audibly to the blessed Virgin to protect us. We prayed also, knowing our lives had never been more in the hands of God than when flying in a decrepit and overloaded plane across the Amazon. It was a relief when we splashed down and began our overland journey to Manizales.

It was night when the train chugged its way around the sides of the Andes and we glimpsed the lights of Manizales on the mountainside. After living in a town with no electricity, the incandescence of Manizales was a beautiful sight.

We were surprised to discover that the pastor lived in the church. The chapel was surrounded on all sides with small rooms, two of which were bedrooms and another was a kitchen. On Sunday, the rooms were used for Sunday school classes, but during the week we lived in them. The furniture was sparse, and it was not cozy, but it was our home for four months.

Since it was December, we began preparation for the Christmas program. I put an old sewing machine to use making costumes. For music practice, there was my accordion. In the eighth month of my pregnancy, that was an accomplishment! Knowing that our baby could be born any day, we worked hard to have everything in readiness for the program.

Labor began December 13. That was also the day

we discovered a broken sewer pipe under the house. Our water was shut off all day while George and two church members worked desperately to fix the break. They completed the job at six o'clock. An hour later, our darling little Sylvia Ruth was placed in my arms. I had prayed for a girl, and my heart overflowed with joy as I held her.

David, now a sophisticated nine-year-old, arrived home from the Alliance Academy and joyfully welcomed his baby sister. Joey, who acted as though a new baby was an everyday occurrence, kissed her and ran out to play.

Since Sylvia was born at home, the mission sent one of its nurses, Aleura Allen, who gave me a week's assistance. By December 20, I was again practicing for the Christmas program, and on December 23, we presented it to the people.

After the program, we transformed the platform into our living room, with a Christmas tree at one corner. Fortunately, there was a rocking chair in the house, and it was a pleasure to sit in it as I nursed the baby. How can I forget our living room on the platform of a church! A couple of old chairs, the glow of the Christmas tree, two boys playing with their toys, a beautiful baby girl in my arms, and the love of a wonderful husband and dad overshadowing us all— that was our special Christmas in Manizales.

The warmth of family love made the sparse setting a happy contrast to the rows of darkened pews in the auditorium beyond the edge of the platform. Our togetherness as a family complete was our special gift.

A week after Christmas we prepared to send David and Joey to Quito. George would accompany the two boys. I remember Joey, all dressed up for the trip, sitting on my lap at the airport waiting for the time to leave. I wanted only to hold my little boy, and he willingly sat there, feeling the excitement of a plane trip, but reluctant to go. He could not know what it meant to me to send away our six-year-old. He was chubby, rosy-cheeked and beautiful, and my heart ached for him as he and his brother and father mounted the steps of the plane.

Holding my little Sylvia, I cried as I pondered the cost of missionary life. The constant changes, the giving up of our rights to our children, the hazards to our health, the loneliness for relatives whose lives went on without us, the thoughts of dear friends who no longer kept in contact—it was overwhelming. But after the tears, I thanked God for the privilege of being a mother and of having children to place at Jesus' feet. I thanked Him for a missionary husband who lived entirely for bringing lost people to Christ. And I thanked God for the many people whom we had had the privilege of winning from darkness to light. While my human nature grieved, my spiritual nature praised the God who had called us to serve Him.

Three months later, we were on our way back across the Andes to the edge of the jungle. There we hired a huge dugout and began our trip homeward. Tiny Sylvia was comfortable in her makeshift bed. Being able to nurse her made travel easier for me. We bathed her in the river to keep her cool. The nights on sand bars were hardest for me. Conscious of the baby beside me under the mosquito net, I could not sleep.

We were disappointed that the dry season had set

in early. We had counted on high water to make a faster trip. Instead, we had to follow the erratic river's channel, which took days longer.

After five days, I became ill with dysentery. I became so weak that when we arrived at a small naval base, George requested a plane to take us home. The officers kindly gave me medicine for my ailment and arranged for a flight to Leguizamo. With great gratitude we flew across the jungle, looking down on the curvaceous river that otherwise would have been our slow highway.

When we landed at Leguizamo, the primitive village looked good to us both. I was so ill I wanted only to get into my own bedroom. The pastor and his wife who had been occupying our house accommodated with grace. They also continued to care for the household duties until their boat left a week later.

I was recovering, but little Sylvia became very ill. For days we prayed that the illness would pass. There was no doctor, but the local pharmacist diagnosed her trouble as an allergy, undoubtedly from the drugs I was taking. I stopped them at once, but Sylvia was very sick. The skin began to peel from her body in handfuls. Her fever was high. Night after night, I walked the floor with her. There was no one to turn to but God.

As I paced back and forth, watching her baby face by candlelight, I kept singing every verse of "Great Is Thy Faithfulness" until the song has been forever etched in my memory. Over and over we committed tiny Sylvia to the Lord's mercy and oh! how we praised Him when she began to mend.

CHAPTER
15

# Up and Down the River

THE STEADY ROAR OF THE OUTBOARD motor droned
on hour after hour, pushing our dugout toward
home. It had been inspiring and refreshing to attend
the annual missionary conference. But with the long
days of river travel, our weary bodies ached for the
comforts of home, and we wondered if it had been
worth the effort. It was mid-afternoon, and the sun
would soon be descending toward its brief twilight.

Suddenly, the sound of the motor changed, then
died. We grabbed paddles and rowed to the river
bank. There George cut banana leaves and carefully
laid out the parts of the motor as he studied the
problem. While he worked, I climbed the steep bank
and saw a hut built on stilts. A lone Huitoto Indian
stood beside the hut, watching us apprehensively.

Needing a break, George joined me. As we approached the old Indian, we waved a greeting, but he
did not respond. At first we thought his reluctance
was because he did not speak Spanish. He assured
us, however, that he understood and spoke Spanish.
He simply wanted no dealings with white men.

Our smiles and our evident interest in him broke

down the man's resistance somewhat. He listened as we told the story of God's great salvation and His love, of blood that would cleanse sin and fit him for heaven. As we talked about Jesus, the Indian kept shaking his old head.

In reply, he began to tell us of the awful atrocities he had lived through during the earlier years of our century. With the advent of the motor car in America and Europe, industrialists were desperate for enough rubber for tires and other components. With bitterness he related how evil men had tortured the Indians in order to get the coveted rubber.

Gazing out across the jungle, he told how his wife and sons were beaten until the blood flowed. He pointed to the scars on his legs and indicated that such scars covered his entire body.

At first the white men gave the Indians machetes and trinkets. But when all the trees along the river's edge were bled, the Indians were forced to penetrate deeper into the jungle for latex. The Indians lived a simple life of hunting and fishing, and they had no need for money. They became unhappy with the disruption of their tribal life. It was when the Indians refused to comply that the terrible brutality began. They were ordered to bring rubber—or else! Each Indian was assigned a quota, and if he returned at sunset without having filled it, his wife and children were beaten or killed before his eyes. If a desperate Indian vanished silently into the jungle night or committed suicide, his wife and children were tortured as a lesson to others. The lash of the horrible bullwhip produced screams in the night and announced to every member of the tribe that it did not pay to disobey.

It mattered not that sick Indians trembled with malarial fevers. They had to endure the splitting headaches and cold sweats, the leeches and ticks clinging to their legs, the flies that lay eggs under the skin. The morning swim that was a part of Indian life became only a memory, for before daybreak they were herded into the forest in quest of rubber. At night, exhausted and filthy, they were not permitted to plunge into the cool waters lest they end their misery beneath the soothing flow.

Driven by the white bosses and desperate to fill their quota, they had no time to watch for deadly snakes. At night, huddled together like animals in filthy shelters, they could only whisper of the horror of their lives and dream of bygone days when they lived in their own huts with their wives and children and knew the peace and beauty of tribal life.

We were shocked as we listened to the old Indian's story. We had picked up snatches of similar stories from others up and down the river, but it was always what had happened to a deceased father or grandfather. Here was one who had actually endured the long ordeal. We could understand why he would never trust a white man again, much less accept the white man's religion. Our words to him were in vain.

Frequently we hear complaints that Protestant missionaries disrupt the lives of primitive peoples when they enter their areas with the gospel. All too often — and certainly in Latin America — it has not been missionaries who have spoiled the primeval tribes. We missionaries have arrived later — to weep over the injustices and to do what we can to rectify the wrongs.

George found the trouble with the motor, and

soon we were once more gliding along the waterway, now shadowed by the late afternoon sun. Our hearts were heavy as we swept past the blue-green forests where millions of rubber trees had enticed greedy men, bribed by exorbitant salaries, to bring out rubber "at any price."

One day we left Leguizamo early in the morning to visit some families living about three hours by motorized dugout from our home. A few miles of the journey was on the Putumayo River, but the rest was on a smaller tributary. We took only provisions for the day, for we expected to be home by sundown. Sylvia was with us, comfortable in her improvised bed-playpen made from a crate that once had contained Bibles.

It was a lovely morning, and the jungle freshness was a delight. Our motor hummed along at a good speed, and before noon we arrived at our destination and were enthusiastically welcomed by those we had gone to see. We spent three hours explaining the gospel and answering questions, then started back, expecting to be home by late afternoon.

The narrower tributary was a blessing in the early afternoon. With less open space, we enjoyed more shade from the scorching midday sun. We realized that we were absolutely alone in that long stretch of jungle, but the tranquility of the area and the joy of sowing the seed of truth in hungry hearts left no room in our minds for anxiety.

Suddenly, the hum of the motor stopped. I looked back at George. Despair was written on his face. The transom to which the motor was attached had broken loose, sending the motor to the bottom of the river. The dead silence was uncanny.

Fortunately, the damage was high enough on the stern so that no water could enter. We praised God that He had thus protected us from having to spend the night in a jungle filled with snakes, pumas, wild boar and swarms of mosquitoes. With his machete, George cut a tree to mark the spot where the motor went down. Then he handed me a paddle, and we began the bone-wearying job of inching our way toward home.

At first it was not so bad. But as the sun began to set behind the trees and we were still far from the Putumayo River, we felt fear in our hearts. Blackness finally enclosed us. Sylvia slept peacefully, a mosquito net over her box bed. We ate the bananas and cookies we had, but we longed for a cup of coffee. We were thankful for boiled drinking water.

Our arms ached, but hour after hour we paddled through the long night, conscious that a snake could drop from the trees. We could hear the crunch of alligator hides scraping the bottom of the canoe. We praised God for good health and faith in our hearts that He would see us through the ordeal.

Strange noises kept us alert in the blackness of the night. Chattering monkeys swung from tree to tree, their weird calls echoing through the forest as they moved away. Between the exotic calls of birds, the monkey chatter and other sounds, there were periods of dead silence when we reflected on how vulnerable we humans are and how easily our plans can be set aside. We knew there was not another house along that tributary. We hoped someone was praying for us.

It was a relief to hear the birds begin to stir and to see the faint rays of dawn filter through the trees.

Hungry and weary, we welcomed the new day. We felt safe to stretch out in daylight. We found a grassy spot for a half hour of rest. Then on we rowed until at last we came to the Putumayo.

Once on the main river, we hoped to hitch a ride, towed by a boat or a motorized canoe. But there was no activity. At least we could praise God for a contented baby who played in her sheltered box as though nothing was wrong. Hour after hour we rowed, reaching Leguizamo about noon.

The next day, after repairing the dugout and borrowing a motor, George looked for a diver. He found an Indian famous for his ability to endure deep-water pressure. After three hours of travel, they located the marked spot where the motor had gone down.

First, they had to cut, trim and implant a sapling in mid-stream as an anchor for the dugout. It would also provide a pole to cling to while they descended in search of the motor. A long rope with a piece of iron on the end provided a sounding device. After hours of probing, they heard the "ting" of metal on metal, and the diver prepared to descend.

As a precaution against the alligators, electric eels and piranha fish known to be in the area, they set off a stick of dynamite. Knowing the dangers of the venture, the Indian had negotiated a price for his services. But when he was ready to go over the side, he looked at George and said, "I go down only if you go with me!"

That had not been part of the bargain! But George realized he had no choice. The Indian went down first and George followed, pushing himself downward on the pole. He held his breath as long as possible, then came up for air. The Indian stayed down longer, but he also surfaced without having secured the motor. After many attempts, the Indian was able to tie the rope to the motor and they pulled it to the surface.

It would have been easier to have counted the motor a loss, but George could not give up without a try. It was a happy George who returned home with the motor he had lost. After a thorough cleaning, it served for the rest of our term in the jungle.

By our last year in the Amazon, the area was enjoying an influx of colonists from the cities. People living in the squalor of city slums were taking a chance on jungle life and the offer of free land. Leguizamo was growing, and up and down the Putumayo new villages were springing up. Small stores, bakeries and new businesses were making life easier for everyone.

Instead of vast distances between settlements, we could now minister with much less travel between points. We spent much time traveling the river, taking the gospel to these transplanted city people. We dreamed of church expansion once we returned from furlough. We had been led by the Spirit of God to the jungle, and we expected to spend the rest of our missionary lives in the development of churches in that neglected area.

## Good-bye Forever

The sun was sinking in the west
   And the afternoon shadows fell
On the face of an old, old Indian
   A century had marked so well.

He sat by his bamboo cottage
  And thought of the years gone by—
Years he wished he could forget
  As he waited now to die.

He lifted his eyes to the river
  As he heard the familiar roar
Of another outboard motor
  That would pass close by his door.

The roar of those noisy motors
  He wished he never knew.
He loved the sound of dripping paddle
  Guiding silently his canoe.

A dugout with outboard motor
  Stopped near the old man's door
And he watched with apprehension
  As a white man came ashore.

He did not respond as the stranger
  Waved in a friendly way;
When the man drew near, the Indian
  Had nothing at all to say.

Yes, he understood Spanish,
  Though he spoke it brokenly,
But he would not talk with the white man
  But sat there stubbornly.

While the white man told about Jesus
  And how He had come to die
That the Indian might have eternal life
  In a home beyond the sky.

He shook his head as the white man
  Told of Christ's death for sin
And how God could change a wicked life
  And put love and peace within.

And then, with frustration and anger
 The Indian spoke at last;
He said he did not believe it
 And could prove it false from his past.

"Long ago," he said, "in the forest
 We were happy, peaceful, free;
With our jungle trails and dugouts,
 Our tribe and family.

"But the white man came and enslaved us
 And sent us to forest trails
For rubber—as much as he ordered—
 Or death to the one who would fail.

"I tried so hard to get plenty,
 But my quota I could not fill;
They said the tribe was just lazy
 And to teach us, they had to kill.

"So my wife and my sons were beaten
 Till the blood on the ground ran red,
And my brother was horribly tortured
 Until at last, he was dead.

"And I cannot forget my young daughter—
 Just 14 and sweet and shy.
They beat her until she crawled away
 To the forest alone to die.

"In the jungle, searching for rubber,
 I wanted to take my life,
But they said, 'For every dead Indian,
 There is torture and death for his wife.'

"When at last the white man departed,
 Just a few of the tribe remained—
Disheartened, discouraged, defeated,
 Our souls with hatred stained.

"You talk to me about Jesus
 And I remember only the boss
Who ordered his men to beat us, yet
 He wore on his neck—a cross!

"The lash of the horrible bullwhip,
 The memory of screams in the night,
And when the torture was over,
 To the Virgin they lit a light.

"Every act, every deed of cruelty,
 We noted with growing despair,
Ended by making the sign of the cross—
 'Twas the symbol they used in prayer.

"White man, don't talk to me of a cross,
 Don't tell me it takes away sin,
For the scars I bear on my body
 Prove the cross makes beasts of men.

"And love—did you speak to me of love?
 The only love I remember today
Is the love of my tribe and family
 Which you and your cross took away!

"Too late, white man, is your message,
 Too late this poor soul to save.
I've known only cruelty and hatred,
 And with this I go to my grave.

"But look, white man, look up river
 And see there is tribe after tribe
Of Indians who never yet have known
 This beautiful love you describe.

"You say the wonderful Book you bring
 Is just what we Indians need.
But no one has ever cared enough
 To teach my people to read.

"Young Indians know my sad story,
    But my path they never trod;
So perhaps since their hearts are not bitter
    They'll believe in the love of your God.

"Perhaps to the young generation
    You might prove that a God above
Sent His Son to die for the Indian
    If you show him a cross — of love!

"Good-bye, good-bye, Mr. White Man!
    Take your canoe away from my shore.
I'm old and I'm tired of living,
    *Adios* — forever more!"

                                    Helen Constance

CHAPTER

16

# *Cali*

WE LEFT LEGUIZAMO AND THE Amazon jungle fully expecting to return after our year's furlough in the United States. Two cablegrams from Colombia changed our plans totally.

The first informed us that George had been elected field director. The unanimous vote, subsequently ratified by the homeland board, meant that we would live in the city of Cali, where the headquarters of the Colombian Alliance Mission was located. Instead of steamy jungle, Cali was at a springtime altitude of 3,000 feet. Instead of a dugout canoe, we would use a car. Instead of muddy streets, there were paved, tree-lined avenues. Instead of beans and rice, there was a market with luscious fruits and vegetables. Instead of isolation, there would be a steady stream of visitors and guests. Quito was a brief 90-minute flight for our school children.

But George had always felt called to pioneer work. We asked for time to consider. And that was when the second cablegram came.

The second cable informed us that the town of Leguizamo had been destroyed by fire. It started when a thatch roof caught fire while a woman was frying food. It swept like a holocaust through the rows of tinder-dry grass homes. People had managed to save our refrigerator, but nearly everything else was lost.

With home and chapel gone, we felt God had given us His answer. George accepted the position of field director.

If living conditions in Cali were pleasant, the administrative work was more demanding than anything we had encountered either in the mountains or the jungle. I say "we," because in those days there was no secretary assigned to the headquarters office. In addition to all my other responsibilities, I was George's secretary.

The year 1950 marked the beginning of a decade of bloody civil war in Colombia known as *La Violencia*. The two political parties, the liberal intellectuals who wanted to see a separation of church and state and the church-controlled Conservatives, became locked in a fanatical power struggle that cost an estimated 200,000 lives—some say more. The Catholic clergy, aligned with the Conservatives, encouraged the military to use the war to stamp out Protestantism in Colombia, especially in the remote rural areas where the gospel was flourishing.

The early policy of the Alliance had been to bypass the urban centers where mainline Protestant denominations had established churches. Instead, we went where the gospel had not yet penetrated. Usually that meant rural areas such as Neiva, Gigante and Leguizamo and the scattered settlements farther into the hills or the jungle. Entire communities were transformed through the saving power of Jesus Christ. Religious holidays that once had been orgies of drunkenness and debauchery became gospel celebrations marked by evangelistic meetings and baptisms.

Now these believers were the special target of the unmitigated violence that was swirling throughout Colombia. We were shocked when we first received word that our churches had been burned and our pastors killed. In some places, entire families were wiped out. The soldiers, heartless and vicious, horse-whipped groups of believers down mountain trails, caring not for their hunger and exhaustion. Many died outright. The weak were left to the wild beasts. Some were able to escape to the hills, each to fend for himself or herself. Family members lost track of each other.

When complaints of this violence were brought to government officials, they dismissed them as the normal fallout of war rather than the persecution it was.

We missionaries knew the price our people were paying to be evangelical Christians. We spent wakeful nights and sorrowful days agonizing over their plight. All of us gave much of our modest allowances to help the widows and orphans and the families of those imprisoned for their Christian testimony.

Because most of the violence was in the rural areas, people flocked to the cities by the thousands. Many times, in the midst of office work, we would answer a knock on our door to find a mother and her children, hungry and destitute, seeking help. It was a privilege to share with them and to help them find jobs.

The influx of believers enabled George and me and the Bob Searings to do something we considered important—we began an Alliance church in Cali. And over the years that central church in Cali has given birth to a number of daughter churches. I had a Sunday school class for teenage girls. It grew until some 25 girls were attending—most of them victims of *La Violencia*. Many of them did not know where their families or other relatives were.

We had a passing acquaintance with a number of wealthy Americans who lived in Cali. Invariably, they were frustrated by the thieving and deceit of their domestic help. So I began to recommend to them my Christian Sunday school girls who needed employment. As the word spread that our Protestant girls could be trusted, we had no trouble finding work for all who wanted jobs. Once a week I invited these working girls to our house. Over homemade treats from my kitchen, we studied the Word, shared experiences and prayed together.

After dealing with all the problems caused by this time of upheaval, what a blessing our Sylvia was to us! After the boys, with their cars, trucks, marbles and erector sets, it was a pleasure to watch her care for her dolls like a little mother. She was as dainty as a flower, and it was fun to dress her in ruffles and ribbons. Such a cuddly, loving little girl was God's special gift to us at that difficult time.

The persecution also served to bring together the many evangelical missions and missionaries working in Colombia. Fellowship between missionaries was closer and more spiritual than ever before as we prayed together for Colombian Christians of all denominations. To present a united front before the government, an association of evangelicals was organized.

Missionaries in the rural areas carried on their work as best they could. The American embassy let it be known that it could not guarantee the safety of Americans who chose to be outside the major cities.

One day, a letter arrived at the office from evangelicals in Campo Hermoso telling of the tragedies in that area. Soldiers had killed the pastor and burned their church. They had razed homes and violated the women. Many of the members had fled into the mountains to hide. The letter ended with a question: "Will the mission abandon us in our time of desperate need?"

George read the letter, then bowed his head on his arms at his desk. I tiptoed out of the room. A half hour later, George emerged red-eyed from the office. "I have to go to them," he announced resolutely.

My first reaction was to protest. Surely enough people were being killed without my husband putting himself in such a vulnerable position. But understanding the need to let the suffering believers know that we were supportive of them, I could only ask that he make sure of God's will.

The next day, as I kissed George good-bye, I wondered if I would ever see him again. For the next three weeks, while George was gone, the newspapers were filled with terrible tales of atrocities. In one documented story, sunrise had revealed a whole row of human heads impaled on a picket fence on the edge of one town. Such accounts kept people in a state of fear. My heart cried out to God for my husband's safety even as I consoled many widows who had lost theirs.

It was a glad day when a disheveled George appeared at the mission door. He could hardly wait to get in the shower and then sit down to a square meal. For three weeks he had slept wherever there was shelter, eaten whatever was available and lived each day with sorrow for his fellow believers' anguish. We talked far into the night as he reported the awful devastation caused by the civil war.

George had traveled from Cali by train, then taken a bus to the point where a believer waited with horses and accompanied him into the mountains. George was appalled to see that home after home along the trail had been burned to the ground. Miraculously, one house was still standing. Upon greeting him, the family fanned out to inform those in hiding to come. Hours later they filled the house. For most of the night George listened to the tales of heartbreak and cruelty. Many who had escaped were living in makeshift shelters deep in the mountains.

The people wept and prayed together, and George consoled them from the Word of God. Then, as dawn broke over the mountains, one man went with George to the site of their church, which had been destroyed by fire. Only a small part of one wall remained standing. With saddened hearts, the two men prayed for the scattered congregation.

Returning again to the believer's home, George proposed that the mission provide blankets, cooking utensils and food for those in hiding as well as anyone else in need. To his surprise, the leader thanked him but wanted any available money to go to the rebuilding of their church. George was humbled. In the midst of their personal destitution, their priority was their church.

One night, while George was staying in the home of evangelicals, four armed soldiers suddenly appeared at the door and demanded that he accompany them to a cliff at the edge of the village. Obviously, it would be an ideal place to quietly eliminate an evangelical leader. Miraculously, the soldiers allowed one of the believers to accompany George.

In the silence of the night, the two men marched ahead of their four captors on the lonely Andes trail. Both men's hearts were pounding as they thought of their loved ones and prayed for deliverance.

All at once, the other man touched George's arm and motioned to the left. "*Vamos!* Let's go!" he whispered. The two bolted down a side trail in the moonlight, then through a field and woods as fast as they could run, to the home where George's horse was tied. Desperately they saddled the animal, expecting any moment that the soldiers would appear in pursuit. Following directions down another trail, accompanied for a while by his running companion, George hurried his mount as he praised the Lord for protection in that critical hour.

As I listened to George's story of suffering believers, I could not help but wonder, as the saintly Job had wondered millenniums earlier, why the righteous suffer. And why had my husband been spared when other Christian men were killed before the eyes of their families in Colombia's blood bath? One thing was certain: both of us knew we would never be the same.

It was in that time of mental and emotional stress that God took us through a personal Gethsemane. We received a radiogram from Quito informing us that Joey was seriously ill and advising us to come at once. George rushed to the embassy for the necessary papers, only to learn that Colombia had been declared in a state of siege. All borders were closed; there was no movement into or out of the country. That night another radiogram arrived reporting that Joey's crisis would be either that night or the next day. Frustrated at not being able to go to Joey and disconsolate in our sorrow, we committed our son once again to God, rededicated our own lives and asked for the gift of intercession. It was a long night of prayer.

Dawn brought the reassuring view of the incredible snowcapped Andes. It was also a fiesta day, and already people were in the streets celebrating, some of them drunk even at that early hour. We waited impatiently for further news from Quito.

How full of praise we were when word came that Joey had passed the crisis and all was well. Years later, in a women's retreat in the United States, Alice Forward, a missionary to Ecuador, shared the story of how as house parents at the Alliance Academy, she and her husband, Roy, had carried the burden when Joey Constance hung between life and death with spinal meningitis. We were profoundly grateful to these two who had been mother and father to our son when his own parents were denied a place at his side.

With renewed dedication, we gave ourselves to the suffering, sorrowing people around us. God had assured us that He was able to care for our absent children. Meanwhile, the experience gave us a new empathy for the hurting Colombian believers.

## Take Thou My Place

Dear Lord, in secret prayer I weep
   And clutch a cable in my hand
That tells me how my little son
   Lies ill and in a distant land
While I, Thy missionary, Lord,
   Lift now my anxious heart to Thee
In fervent prayer that Thou wilt heal
   The little boy so dear to me.

The cable tells me that tonight
   Will be the crisis for our son.
Don't let him die, dear Lord, I pray,
   But let a miracle be done.
Forgive the bitter tears I shed
   Because there was no way to go
To my sick boy. Oh, Lord, forgive —
   Thou knowest that I love him so!

I think how Christian mothers, Lord,
   So far away in my homeland,
Can sit beside their little ones
   And dry the tears with loving hand.
Those mothers love Thee as I do,
   And yet no price like mine they pay,
So help them now to hear Thy voice;
   Compel them, Lord, just now to pray.

I knew, when to my breast I held
   My tiny babe in years gone by,
That he was mine for just six years,
   Then I would have to say good-bye.
And now he's far away and ill,
   And I cannot be by his bed
To pour out all my mother love
   And hold his fevered, aching head.

Through blinding tears I see beyond
    The window where I've knelt to pray
The mountains reaching up to God
    As I am reaching, Lord, today.
The Andes loom against the sky,
    And 'round their purple, ragged peaks
Are glorious, golden rainbow hues,
    And from that beauty, Thou dost speak:

"If thou would take thy rugged cross
    And follow me to sinful men,
Then thou must break the closest ties
    With mother, father, child or friend."
I thought that I had yielded all
    The day I bravely waved good-bye
And sent my little boy away.
    Yet, crushed and broken now, I cry.

For Satan's subtle whispers say,
    "You could have him at your side;
If you had served the Lord at home,
    Your little child might not have died."
Beyond my window now I hear
    Fiesta-drunken beings wild—
The souls that I may win if I
    Will meekly sacrifice my child.

There is no one to take my place,
    There is no way for me to leave,
So I accept Thy holy will—
    Thy precious Word I still believe.
For Thou hast promised, Lord, to be
    With us always, so I pray,
Stand beside my darling's bed
    And touch and heal my boy today.

No sacrifice would be too great
    If I from hell lost souls can win

To Thee, who saved my own lost soul
    From hopeless, wayward paths of sin.
People trapped in darkest night,
    Stumbling on in sin and shame,
Have never known the beauty or
    The power of Thy wondrous name.

Children sick and dying need
    My love, my motherly embrace,
So help me give my love to them
    While Thou, Dear Lord, dost take my place.
I will not beg that I might leave
    Thy whitened harvest field and go
Where Joey is, but this request
    Thou wilt now grant to me, I know:

Take Thou my place and whisper low
    Of Thy great and tender love divine,
And fill his heart with peace and heal
    That precious little boy of mine.
Hold *Thou* his hand and in his heart
    Implant Thy sweet and wondrous grace;
Thy love is greater far than mine,
    So, Lord, please take my place.

                                    Helen Constance

# "If I Were Young Again"

IT WAS IN THE MIDST OF Colombia's civil war that George and I received a disturbing cable from our homeland headquarters. It informed us that George had been unanimously chosen to be regional director of Christian and Missionary Alliance work in Africa, the Middle East and Latin America.

We were shocked! We had been so preoccupied with our own crisis situation in Colombia that we had hardly had time to think about other parts of the world. George and I looked at each other in astonishment. Leave Colombia at a time when our people most needed us?

Letters from relatives and friends bearing newspaper clippings about the violence in Colombia had long urged us to leave. But for George, as director of the mission, the thought of leaving in the midst of disaster was unthinkable. His attitude was unaltered.

So it did not take George long to write a letter explaining that a change of ministry at that time was ill-advised. Two weeks later, we received a letter stating that the board could not accept our decision.

Convinced that the Holy Spirit had led them to the right person for the job, they asked George to pray about it and reconsider.

We were filled with confusion. We thought about the civil war and the plight of our people and wondered how we could bring ourselves to abandon them at such a time. We had supposed that our call to Colombia was for life. It had never occurred to us that the Lord might have another plan.

In the end, and with great reluctance, George agreed to the new position, and we made plans to leave. Once again we broke up another home that was dear to us. Packing was easy. We gave almost everything we had either to missionaries or to Colombian Christians. But it was difficult to walk away from the nearly three terms of missionary work we loved.

George kissed me good-bye and left for New York. The next day I flew to Quito to help at the Academy until school was out in May.

It was an exciting day when we stopped in front of what would be our new home in Nyack. Built on a hillside, its front door was reached by descending 22 steps from the street. More steps led to the garage on another level behind the house. We wondered how we would cut the grass on such steep banks.

A call from George's brother-in-law, Otto Bublat, pastor of the Alliance church in Hartford, Connecticut, resolved our need for furniture. A woman in his church had just refurbished her home and would gladly give us her used furniture. We felt like millionaires as we placed the sofa and chairs in the empty living room and arranged the dining room and bedrooms. We appreciated the generosity of the Hart-

ford parishioner and the efforts of those who
brought the furniture to us.

George's work meant daily commuting to his office in New York City when he was home—which
was seldom. In addition to long trips abroad, he had
conventions and weekend assignments that left little
time for family. It seemed as though we were either
waving good-bye as he left or waiting at the airport to
welcome him home.

To my surprise, I, too, was invited to speak at wom-
en's meetings, missionary conventions and at many
churches. It was a busy life and often, without a
husband to help, I felt exhausted and discouraged.
But once I stood behind those pulpits made for tall
people, the presence of God would fill my soul, and I
felt His anointing. Back home again, the mountain
of work waited and took precedence over correspon-
dence with missionary friends.

It was a delight to enjoy the special events in our
children's lives. Joe (he was no longer Joey) was playing high school soccer, and I went to as many games
as possible. I sat spellbound as he played his trumpet
in school and church. Sylvia kept in perpetual motion in choir, Bible Memorization League, summer
camps, piano and flute. I found myself enrolled in
one of David's classes at Nyack College. A strong
enthusiasm for life dominated our home as the children came and went from one activity to another,
often barely passing their parents en route. As missionaries, we could only imagine the special events in
our children's lives. We praised God for the precious
years together before they left home.

And now, it is much, much later. George rounded

out 18 years of service as regional director before retiring at the end of 1971. Never one to sit still, he became interim pastor of a number of Alliance churches, most of them in Florida, where we now live. Both of us continue to be active with speaking engagements.

David is now a missionary—to Argentina, where he and his wife have served since 1963. Joe has a doctorate in political science and has been involved in college administration.

Sylvia awaits us in heaven. The day before her graduation from high school in Nyack, New York, in 1965, a routine chest X-ray revealed some abnormal lumps that proved to be the onset of Hodgkin's disease. Amid radiation treatments, back pain and severe headaches, Sylvia struggled through college. On June 13, 1970, she became the wife of seminarian James McGarvey, and together they served the Alliance Church of Kissimmee, Florida. On January 22, 1975, not quite 10 full years from the first discovery of cancer, Sylvia Constance McGarvey entered the Lord's presence. Two parents, grateful to God for entrusting such a joy and blessing to them, look forward fondly to the coming reunion.

On different occasions, after I have spoken in behalf of missions, young people have come up to me with a question. If you could be young again, they ask, having had the experiences you have had and knowing what you know about missionary life, would you choose the mission field?

Our lives have been more full and varied than most people's. We rode the rugged trails of the Andes, we traveled the Amazon rivers in dugouts. We tramped the busy streets of Colombian cities. We have known danger and persecution for Christ's sake. We have been separated from our children. But having experienced all that, we look back over a long and contented lifetime and can honestly say that if God gave us the opportunity, we would not do it differently!

### If I Were Young

If I could just be young again,
　And if I had the choice
To be a multimillionaire
　Or have a famous voice;
If I could have rare beauty or
　The best vocabulary,
I'd turn my back on all those things
　And be a missionary.

If I could have the wisdom of
　An Einstein if I chose;
If I could have great talent
　Or wear the finest clothes;
If I could choose to see the world,
　I would not fear or tarry.
I'd say good-bye to all those things
　And be a missionary.

If I could just be young again,
　I'd yield to Christ my all;
At early age I'd answer yes
　To Jesus' loving call,
Then say good-bye to home and friends—
　My other dreams I'd bury—
And follow Christ to lands afar
　And be His missionary.

I'd walk the dusty city streets
　　Where unsaved millions live,
I'd tell the gospel of my Lord—
　　My time, my love I'd give.
I'd travel jungle rivers in
　　Canoe if necessary,
Or live a life that's primitive,
　　But be a missionary.

I'd ride the hardest mountain trail
　　O'er rugged Andes peak,
Or follow Christ if He should lead
　　To deserts hot and bleak.
I would not trade the privilege
　　To tell the gospel story
For all the world could offer me
　　Of pleasures, wealth or glory.

To see a never-dying soul
　　Confess to Christ his sin,
Then watch him live a transformed life
　　Before his fellowmen
Brings joy into the human heart
　　And makes the angels sing;
It gives the missionary peace
　　The world can never bring.

What if the sun does burn my brow
　　If children I can teach?
What if I'm drenched by jungle rain
　　If gospel truth I preach?
What if I cannot have the food
　　That once was customary
If I can give the Bread of Life
　　And be Christ's missionary!

The millions longing for the truth
　　In false religions search

While Jesus waits for us to help
    Establish His true church.
If I were young, I'd choose a life
    Like Livingstone or Carey!
And though my light would fainter shine,
    I'd be a missionary.

                             Helen Constance

| DATE DUE | | | |
|---|---|---|---|
| | | | |
| | | | |
| | | | |
| | | | |
| | | | |
| | | | |
| | | | |
| | | | |
| | | | |
| | | | |
| | | | |
| | | | |